YOUNG PEOPLE IN POST-COMMUNIST RUSSIA AND EASTERN EUROPE

Young People in Post-Communist Russia and Eastern Europe

Edited by

PROFESSOR JAMES RIORDAN
Chair of Russian Studies
University of Surrey, Guildford

DR CHRISTOPHER WILLIAMS
Lecturer
University of Central Lancashire, Preston

PROFESSOR IGOR ILYNSKY
Rector
Institute of Youth Studies, Moscow, Russian Federation

Dartmouth

Aldershot • Brookfield USA • Singapore • Sydney

Published by
Dartmouth Publishing Company Limited
Gower House
Croft Road
Aldershot
Hants GU11 3HR
England

Dartmouth Publishing Company
Old Post Road
Brookfield
Vermont 05036
USA

British Library Cataloguing in Publication Data
Young People in Post-Communist Russia and
Eastern Europe
   I. Riordan, James
   362.70947

Library of Congress Cataloging-in-Publication Data
Young people in post-communist Russia and Eastern Europe / edited by
  James Riordan, Christopher Williams, Igor Ilynsky.
     p.   cm.
    Essays presented at a conference on "The problems facing
contemporary Russian and Eastern Europe youth" at the Institute of
Youth Studies, Moscow, in late November 1993.
    Includes bibliographical references and index.
    ISBN 1-85521-672-8
    1. Youth–Europe, Eastern–Social conditions–Congresses.
  2. Youth–Russia (Federation)–Social conditions–Congresses.
  3. Post-communism–Europe, Eastern–Congresses. 4. Post-communism-
-Russia (Federation)–Congresses. I. Riordan, James, 1936-
II. Williams, Christopher, 1959-   . III. Ilynsky, Igor' Mikhailovich.
HQ799.E92Y68   1995
305.23'5'0947–dc20   95-30982
                                                CIP

ISBN 1 85521 672 8

Printed and bound in Great Britain by
Hartnolls Ltd, Bodmin, Cornwall

Contents

List of tables

Notes on contributors

Editors

James Riordan is Head of the Department of Linguistic and International Studies and Professor of Russian Studies at the University of Surrey. He studied and worked in the Soviet Union for five years and has written extensively on Soviet sport, youth and Russian society. His most recent works include *Soviet Youth Culture* (1992); *Soviet Social Reality in the Mirror of Glasnost* (1992); *Dear Comrade Editor: Letters to the Editor During Perestroika* (with Sue Bridger, 1992) and *Sex and Russian Society* (with Igor Kon, 1993).

Christopher Williams is Lecturer in the Department of European Studies, University of Central Lancashire, Preston. He has published numerous articles on Russian social policy and society in Revolutionary Russia; Irish Slavonic Studies; Journal of Urban History; Sociology of Health and Illness and Northwest Journal of Historical Studies. His first book on *Aids in Post-Communist Russia and its Successor States* was published by Avebury in March 1995. He is currently working on a book about the impact of the transition on Russian society and on a project concerning the Gay and Lesbian movement in the New Europe. He was a visiting Professor at the Institute of Socio-political research, Moscow in March 1994 and a visiting Professor in the Department of Sociology, Belorus State University, Minsk, Belorus in April 1994.

Igor Ilynsky is Rector of the Institute of Youth Studies, Moscow. Professor Ilynsky is a member of the Academy of Pedagogical Sciences and author of numerous articles and books on youth problems. His most recent publications include *Russian Youth: Tendencies, Perspectives* (Moscow 1993) and *The Value World of Contemporary Youth: Towards World Integration* (Moscow, 1994)

Other Contributors

Jacqueline Hennig is a Research Fellow at the Institute of Applied Youth Research, Berlin, Germany.

Bozidar Jaksic is Director of the Institute of Philosophy and Social Theory, Belgrade, Serbia.

Ladislav Machacek is Professor of Sociology, Institute of Sociology, Slovak Academy of Sciences, Bratislava, Slovakia.

Petar-Emil Mitev is President of the Bulgarian Sociology Association, Sofia, Bulgaria.

Boris Ruchkin is Director of the All-Russia Youth Centre, Moscow.

Andrei Sharonov is Chairman of the State Committee on Youth, Moscow.

Larissa Titarenko is Professor of Sociology, Belorussian State University, Minsk, Belorus.

Lydia Yordanova is a Research Fellow, National Public Opinion Centre, Sofia, Bulgaria.

Preface and acknowledgements

This collection of essays was originally presented at a conference on 'The Problems Facing Contemporary Russian and Eastern Europe Youth' at the Institute of Youth Studies, Moscow, Russian Federation in late November 1993. Most have been substantially revised and extended and others have been added in the course of preparation.

The conference was organised by the Institute of Youth Studies, Moscow in conjunction with the Russian State Committee on Youth Affairs. In this context, a special note of thanks goes to Professor Igor Ilynsky, Rector of the Institute of Youth Studies, for inviting a number of distinguished speakers from Britain, Russia and East-Central Europe to attend the conference and to Andrei Sharonov, Chairman of the Russian State Committee on Youth Affairs for providing much needed financial support.

Professor James Riordan, University of Surrey and Dr Christopher Williams, University of Central Lancashire, translated and edited the papers for publication.

Special thanks are also due to Mrs Joanne Kirk and Mrs Tracey Wright who prepared this manuscript for publication.

It is hoped that this survey of the plight of youth in the former Eastern bloc will enable those with an academic or general interest in this region's transition for totalitarianism to liberal democracy to understand just how important it is to put young people as bearers of the future at the top of the political agenda in the New Europe.

Permission to publish

The editors would like to thank Martin and Moira Plant and Routledge Publishers for permission to use a table from *Risk Takers: Alcohol, Drugs, Sex and Youth* (1992) in Chapter 2.

James Riordan, Guildford
Christopher Williams, Preston
Igor Ilynsky, Moscow
April 1995

Abbreviations

CEE	Central and Eastern Europe
CIS	Commonwealth of Independent States
CPSU	Communist Party of the Soviet Union
DDR	German Democratic Republic
ECE	East-Central Europe
FSU	Former Soviet Union
KGB	Committee for State Security
KHOZU UD TsK VLKSM	Economic Department, All-Union Leninist Communist Youth League
KMN	Club of Young unemployed, Slovakia
NAPOC	National Public Opinion Centre, Sofia, Bulgaria

NEP	New Economic Policy
UK	United Kingdom
USSR	Union of Soviet Socialist Republics
VTsIOM	Centre for Public Opinion Research, Moscow
YCL	Young Communist League
YMCA	Young Mens Christian Association

Introduction

The year 1989 marked a watershed not only in East European history, but in world history too. It was one of the most historic moments of modern times, comparable to 1848 or 1917. In one country after another, the ruling regime succumbed in the face of massive popular protest. Poland, Hungary, East Germany, Bulgaria, Czechoslovakia and most dramatically of all, Romania, all saw their communist leaders ousted, new governments installed and contested elections promised or held. Not one of those nations possessed a communist regime by the end of 1990. Of the other two communist East European states, Yugoslavia degenerated into fratricidal civil war and Albanian hard-line communism withered on the bough. Today not only Stalinist communism in Europe is dead, and Leninism is but a twinkle in the eye of a few die-hard communists, but Gorbachovism, which precipitated the 1989 revolutions, was plainly too little, too late.

In each of the East European states, it was young people who pioneered change: they led the strike movement in Poland, they demonstrated for reforms in Hungary, Czechoslovakia and East Germany (where they also tore down the hated Berlin wall), they led the armed insurrection in Romania. Their collective pressure brought down governments, introduced tentative liberal democracy, gained the right to free speech, travel and elections. Even within the Soviet Union, young people played a part in transforming politics, especially in the three Baltic states of Latvia, Lithuania and Estonia.

Such youth inspired revolution was not successful everywhere without bloodshed, as the events in Romania (and, indeed, China) witnessed. Yet, perhaps for the first time in history, virtually the entire world, East and West, reacted in shock and revulsion at the carnage, condemning the oppressions and condoning change. / The very murder of hundreds of young Chinese students by their own government acted as a spur to the successful revolt in the communist nations of Eastern Europe, as if their populations wished to distance themselves from their own history - the abortive uprisings in Poland and East Germany in 1953 and 1954, Hungary and Poland in 1956 and Czechoslovakia in 1968. They seemed determined to put an end to the lies, the hypocrisy, the police surveillance and to Russian *diktat*.

This was a rebellion from below, a unique moment in history when young people took the national stage and made a decisive impact on events. It evoked memories of the year 1968 in the West when so many youthful rebels made the qualitative leap from particular grievances to universal transformation, challenging hierarchy, institutional totems of bourgeois culture, gender, discrimination, racial oppression and the colonisation of everyday life by the state and militarism.

Some two decades later history arrived at the crossroads again. And once more young people were in the vanguard. Could history be repeating itself, this time on the campuses of Russia and Eastern Europe? Similarities abounded: the rebellion against control, bureaucracy and authority; for liberation and self-expression. Yet, as we shall see below, such a comparison is misleading, for the East European struggle was taking place in conditions of dire economic crisis, political bankruptcy and social disorientation.

By contrast with the Western 'crisis of conscience' of the 1960s, however, the economic, political and social circumstances of Russian and East European youngsters could not be more different. In the late 1980s, the old planning and command structure of the economy had broken down; bureaucratic sclerosis had set in; the polity was only tardily emerging from Stalinist totalitarianism, while the citizenry were clamouring impatiently for more voice and participation. Today, several of the former states no longer exist, the old structure has been destroyed, yet no new one has fully taken its place. / What has happened is the dissolution of centres of power, problems and conflicts. In the vacuum that has been created, people, especially the young, have cast off the old ideology and identity, but do not really know where they are going or what to believe in. Therein lies the dilemma.

Now that the economy is everywhere experiencing the problems of adapting to market forces and now that the old polity is bankrupt, the moral code that cemented the old society together is disintegrating. As the Russian sociologist Tatiana Zaslavskaya has written

> Disappointment in socialism is one reason for the crumbling moral foundations. Eternal moral values such as honour, duty, morality and patriotism had been tied to socialist ideology. Now that this ideology is falling apart, people are left without moral guidelines. They no longer know what is good and what is bad[1]

Nor do they know exactly who they are. For many, the now derided *homo sovieticus* (the new socialist personality) was the only positive identification they had. With the disappearance of that identity, they are facing the alarming question: what to believe in? God for many young people is forgotten, Marx, Lenin, Tito, Dmitrov are discredited, communism no longer exists, democracy is an unexperienced abstraction and capitalism attracts some and frightens others. The spiritual crisis goes deep and is causing paralysis throughout society. The only ideology that has appeared in this void is nationalism with all its implicit potential hazards so vividly demonstrated in the aftermath of the Yugoslav communist federation.

If such confusing disorientation is common to adults, it applies even more to young people.

When we look at Russian and East European youth, therefore, we have to see them within the context of the present metamorphosis of their societies. We must also bear in mind that the background of young people differs radically from that of their Western counterparts. Not only are most of them at the earlier stage of modernisation and the 'rural-urban continuum', but most have not experienced inflation and chronic unemployment which are said to be a major source of tension and social ills in the West. This is certainly changing now. Such differences in geographical and social background should warn the Western reader against seeing Russian and East European young people as a mirror image of young Americans, British, French or German youngsters.

Virtually all the chapters in this book started out as papers presented at a Conference on young people at the Moscow Institute of Youth Studies in late November 1993. They address the problems experienced by young people in the transitional period between the old communist regime and the new capitalist society. Clearly, some of these problems may be put down to 'teething troubles' in the course of adaptation; others are more deep-seated and represent as much national, traditional dilemmas as those of an international nature. This is apparent in the approaches by sociologists representing seven of the erstwhile socialist states of Russia and Eastern Europe.

The primary goal of this book is to analyse the position of youth in the former Soviet Union and Eastern Europe. Part One sets the scene by examining the legacy of totalitarianism and the difficulties experienced in making a transition to Western-style liberal democracy, on the one hand and the impact of the latter on the status and perception of youth, on the other.

In Chapter 1, Igor Ilynsky discusses the state of youth in contemporary Russia. This includes a detailed analysis of young people, their health, intellectual development, socio-economic status, crime patterns, attitudes towards politics, present preoccupation's and thoughts about the future.

Christopher Williams points out in Chapter 2 how youth issues have been opened up for public scrutiny. Since 1985, the social ills of Soviet and post-communist Russia have been exposed for all the world to see. Previously taboo subjects, such as alcoholism, drug-abuse, AIDS and crime are now openly debated in the mass media. The same is also true of the problems of young people.

Both Ilynsky and Williams seek to explore how officialdom views youth in the former Soviet Union (hereafter simply FSU) as a social problem. The aim of Part 1 is to show that many youth issues appear in all industrial societies. Thus although some problems of youth are the product of the legacy of Soviet state socialism and negative government perceptions, the post-communist regimes in the FSU and East-central Europe (hereafter ECE) are now facing up to the difficulties of youth. Whether or not the East can learn from Western experience is explored briefly in Chapter 2 and will be reconsidered in the concluding chapter.

In Chapter 3, Petar-Emil Mitev traces the political setting in which current youth policy in the FSU and ECE is taking shape. The obstacles in overcoming the totalitarian legacy are made clear. Mitev stresses that it will be extremely difficult to implement well-defined youth policies at a time of great uncertainty. He concludes by discussing possible future directions for post-Communist states - Americanisation, Europeanisation, Russification, Orientalisation - and by examining the likely impact this will have on the value orientation of and official attitudes towards youth in the FSU and ECE.

Having examined the current degree of governmental and public awareness of the problems facing young people in Part I, various case studies are presented of Russia and the Commonwealth of Independent States (hereafter the CIS) in Part II.

Andrei Sharonov traces the government response to the youth question in Chapter 4. This involves an analysis of the main parameters of youth policy in Russia and the constraints on the implementation of effective policy and decision-making in this sphere.

In Chapter 5, Boris Ruchkin places the plight of youth and current Russian youth policy in its historical perspective. He points out that recent political events have had an adverse effect upon the evolution and development of Russian policies on youth and to a certain extent led to the introduction of an anti-youth policy. The prospects of overcoming these problems are outlined.

James Riordan looks at the past, present and future roles of youth organisations in the Russian Federation in Chapter 6. He demonstrates that under Communism, the Octobrists, Pioneers and the Komsomol were given significant state support. As a result, they were not seen as the true voice of Russian youth. Riordan examines the reasons why these organisations disintegrated by the early 1990s and looks at their fate since the collapse of the Union in late 1991. As he points out, the major problem is that no sizable youth organisations have yet stepped in to fill the vacuum left by the Young Communist League (hereafter YCL). The prospects for the emergence of new youth elites to replace the old communist ideologues is analysed.

The spiritual and cultural crisis among ex-Soviet youth generated by the collapse of the YCL and the communist edifice is addressed by Igor Ilynsky in Chapter 7. He talks of the widespread moral decay in Russia in the 1990s and the lack of direction among many young people - their poor understanding of freedom, lack of faith in politicians, growing sense of injustice and general concerns about what the future might bring. These problems, Ilynsky argues, are being further exacerbated by the clash between the old communist collective values and the rise of individualism as a result of Russia's transition to capitalism. This situation has engendered two problems: generational conflicts and disagreements between young people themselves. The prospects for resolving these difficulties and their impact on future trends are discussed.

Finally in Chapter 8, Larissa Titarenko reviews the situation in Belorus. It is shown that youth in Belorus is facing similar problems to its Russian counterpart. While this is largely a product of the totalitarian legacy, Belorus finds itself in a dilemma - should its government resolve youth problems by seeking the help of its old ally Russia or should it look to the West for assistance? Titarenko clearly demonstrates that youth problems in Minsk and elsewhere in Belorus are similar to many European societies but they are exacerbated by a country undergoing significant transformation.

Finally in Part III, the situation in ECE is considered. A number of case studies are presented of the former Yugoslavia, German Democratic Republic (hereafter DDR), Slovakia and Bulgaria. The goal is to analyse the origins and problems of youth and the driving forces behind the changes which have taken place since the revolutions of 1989.

In Chapter 9, Bozidar Jaksic traces the plight of young people in war-torn Yugoslavia. The current political climate is reviewed and the conflict between factions pushing for 'war' and 'peace' discussed. The attitudes of youth towards this situation and its impact on their status and development are analysed. The long-term effect of the current turmoil on the fate of youth and on ex-Yugoslavia's prospects for recovery by the end of this decade are emphasised.

Jacqueline Hennig examines the impact of German unification on the plight of youth in the former DDR in Chapter 10. She shows that young people are faced with an identity crisis. The initial euphoria of October 1990 has led to a deepening economic recession and political difficulties. Former DDR young people are therefore caught in a dilemma. Not wanting to become second class citizens, many have tried to integrate themselves into their new society. It is shown that only a few have succeeded, with most being subjected to widespread prejudice, hostility and xenophobia.

In Chapter 11, Ladislav Machachek looks at the impact of changes since 1989 on youth organisations in Slovakia. The ability of a variety of ex-communist youth movements to adapt to the changing circumstances is explored. It is shown that like their ex-soviet counterparts (see Chapter 6), new post-communist Slovak youth organisations have been slow to emerge and respond to the new issues arising out of transition to capitalism, such as youth unemployment. It is argued that the Slovak government must step into the vacuum and introduce more appropriate youth policies such as unemployment schemes for school leavers or a safety-net for youth. The obstacles to providing stronger state intervention and/or the development of such measures are discussed.

Finally in Chapter 12, Lydia Yordanova assesses youth values and beliefs in Bulgaria. Emphasising that young people must take an active role in post-communist developments, Yordanova suggests that the future looks bleak in so far as political apathy is widespread among Bulgarian youth. Public opinion survey data are utilised to demonstrate that young people have turned their backs on the state and rely more on their families or peers. Yordanova concludes by arguing that the current disillusionment of youth is having an adverse affect upon Bulgaria's transition to Western-style democracy.

As the contributors to this volume show, the FSU and ECE are experiencing a very difficult transition from totalitarianism to liberal democracy. This is having an adverse effect upon the status and development of youth. Altogether this book provides a unique picture of young people in transition, a perceptive insight into their views of the past, pre-occupations of the present and aspirations for the future.

Part IV seeks to explore possible remedies to the current situation. In this context Igor Ilynsky in Chapter 13 urges academics and policy and decision-makers alike in Russia, and by implication the other ECE countries mentioned here, to put young people first and to reorient their youth policies in a humanist direction. The main aim of which is to allow young people to be the principal factor of change as bearers of the future of Russia, the CIS and ECE. One can only hope that those reading this book will take note of this fact before it is too late.

The concluding chapter points to the fact that the problems outlined in this book exist in many industrial societies. It is suggested, therefore, that East-West co-operation, exchange of information, expertise and above all greater openness about the difficulties faced by young people are essential in helping post-communist regimes rectify past shortcomings and find appropriate solutions to the plight of youth in the FSU and ECE. This book was written with such an objective in mind, after all as James Riordan has noted 'our problems are your problems too'.[2]

Notes

1   Moscow News No. 29, 1990.
2   I. Kon and J. Riordan, *Sex and Russian Society* (London, Pluto Press, 1993), p. 12.

PART I

GENERAL AND COMPARATIVE PROBLEMS

1 The status and development of youth in post-Soviet society

IGOR ILYNSKY

Introduction

During 1992-93, the Research centre, which I headed, in co-operation with other scholarly institutions and social scientists of Moscow, St. Petersburg and other cities of Russia, prepared a report for the President and the government of the country, dealing with the social status and development of youth. Such a report was the first of its kind in the history of Russia. The report covered the main aspects of the life of young people, and was based upon state statistics and sociological surveys.

There is a need to demonstrate that all that is happening in and with Russia today will affect global development. This is precisely why I have decided to reveal the main findings of our study, which until recently have been classified as a state secret, for our conclusions are tinged with tragic colours. Unfortunately, the great bulk of the population of Russia, including the authorities, do not wish to acknowledge the seriousness of the situation, nor understand what awaits Russia if the current processes in the youth environment continue to develop.

Demography

In Russia in 1993, there were about 32 million people aged between 15 and 29. Since 1979 (the year of the last population census), the share of young people has diminished by nearly 15 per cent. Russian society is rapidly dying. The number of marriages is decreasing: in 1981, there were 10.6 marriages per 1,000, in 1991 - 8.6. The number of divorces is growing:- in 1981, there were 570,000 divorces, in 1992 - 620,000. The birth rate is falling sharply: for the first time in the history of Russia, the birth-rate was lower than the death-rate. For example, in 1992, in St. Petersburg, the number of those dying was 2.6 times higher than the number of people born. Maternal and child mortality has also increased. We have direct evidence of a profound crisis in the family, the young family in particular. In conditions of absolute impoverishment of the population, the family has changed to a strategy of physical survival and is obliged to spend nearly all its money on food and clothing, leaving very little for leisure activities and cultural needs. The educational potential of the family, its role in the socialisation of the younger generation, is fast diminishing. The overwhelming majority of families plan to have one child, or two children at most, and this is obviously insufficient even for the reproduction of the population on a simple scale.

The adverse and social consequences of these demographic processes for Russia with its vast territory are self-evident: they will have a deleterious effect on all spheres, including social development and progress as a whole. An ageing society, which is losing its energy and spirit, and which is inclined to conservatism, cannot solve qualitatively new and unfamiliar social problems, the magnitude of which grows continually.

Health and physical development

The tendency for a worsening of the health of young people is patently obvious. Every successive Russian generation of children and teenagers is less healthy than the one before it. Only 14 per cent of Russian children are healthy; 50 per cent have health deviations and 35 per cent have chronic diseases. Only one in five conscripts is fit for military service. The situation is aggravated by the fact that young people, whose health is becoming poorer all the time, are obliged to live and work in constantly deteriorating ecological conditions, which are today recognised to be among the most dangerous in the world. Russia has cities (Magnitogorsk, Novokuznetsk, Nizhny Tagil, Lipetsk, Sterlitamak, Ufa, Angarsk, Kirishi and scores more) where children and teenagers suffer from various diseases as much as ten or even 20 times the norm of children in ecologically 'clean' cities. For example, in Angarsk, 75 per cent of the children have an impaired immunity. The health of children and young people in the coming years will continue to worsen. Incidentally, some of the diseases lead to genetically irreversible processes in the organism. Acute problems of the nation's health have therefore moved from the older to the younger generation into the sphere of childhood and youth, thus endangering the genepool of the Russian nation.

Intellectual development

Youth is the bearer of an enormous intellectual, creative and innovatory potential. In Russia this potential is declining. First of all, this is because of the deteriorating physical and mental health mentioned above. Among young people, the number of mental problems and diseases is growing rapidly and the number of children with mental defects is also rising, which is the consequence, among other things, of the long-term alcoholization of the population. In the five years from 1987 to 1991, the number of mentally retarded children in Russia increased by 16 per cent. Meanwhile hard drinking and alcoholism among young people are gaining momentum. Drug addiction and toxomania are also spreading rapidly. The inadequate diet and malnutrition of many young people will slow down their mental development and lead to protein deficiency and to irreversible processes in the brain.

The *social sources* of reproduction of the intellectual potential are becoming poorer. In the eyes of young people, the value of intellectual labour, education and knowledge continues to fall. State funding for all these needs, which was small in the first place, is being reduced all the time. As a consequence of the growth of social inequality, educational inequality is also growing, thereby narrowing the social base for the development of young people's intellectual potential. As before, the forms and methods of instruction in secondary schools and universities do not favour the development of creative thinking and analysis. Because of low prestige and poor pay, many people engaged in intellectual spheres (scientists, teachers), turn to other spheres of activity without ever realizing themselves as intellectuals. The sphere of intellectual labour is diminishing and 'ageing'. The brain and talent drain has become a serious threat to society. In other words, we are witnessing the intellectual impoverishment and degeneration of the Russian nation.

Economic status

The economic status of young people is as an important element in the productive force of society, but the economic *participation* of young people is extremely low. The dying state economy is unable to use youth labour potential in production. Today only a small minority of young people, comprising a thin layer of business people (2.5 per cent of interviewed persons) and of those intending to engage in business in the future (approximately 20 per cent), is taking part in the process of economic reform. At the same time, new production, which can offer employment to only a few young workers, is struggling to establish itself. The transfer of the most capable and qualified workers and specialists from the state to the private sector is rapidly increasing. However, the majority of young people regard the possibilities of a capitalisation of the economy with distrust and view privatisation as a venture, profitable primarily to the ruling elite and the Mafiosi. In their search for stability (regular work and wages), most young people, following the old traditions, are turning to the state sector, where the possibilities for the economic participation of young people and their role in production management have been reduced to zero. With privatisation, the dissolution of regular economic relations, the reduction in jobs and the closing of state enterprises, conditions no longer exist for youth groups to have any say in how they take part in production.

The decline in the role that the younger generation plays in economic reforms is, first of all, explained by its *attitude to the reforms*. Owing to the numerous mistakes made in the course of the reforms, most young people (40 to 70 per cent depending on the category) have a negative attitude towards reform. Secondly, there is the *attitude of the young towards work* which has, for the majority, lost its meaning as a means of self-assertion and self-realisation. The alienation of young people from work has been taking place for many decades. Today, society has a younger generation which wants to live well and possess everything, but which has neither the desire, nor the ability, to work intensively, honestly and diligently. Many young people do not associate material prosperity with work; what is more, they are prepared to break the law for the sake of money. For the absolute majority of the young, work is meaningless and does not represent a natural component of life. Work is mostly viewed as a necessary evil, a forced action. Such a state of affairs is tragic for both the individual and society. A consequence of the decline of the value of work is the growth in social pessimism and work passivity among young people. For most youngsters, 'real life' begins outside the factory gates since they are primarily oriented on leisure and amusement. The domination of commercial, 'shop' business over production and productive business is largely explained by young people's lack of interest in complex forms of work activity and by the desire to obtain quick and easy money. No 'educational' methods will repair this situation. Young people will have to be put into objective, difficult material conditions where they will have no other choice but to work well and intensively.

Social status

The former relative stability of young people's social position has been roughly destroyed and their social status is rapidly declining on all counts. This is perfectly understandable and, in many ways, unavoidable. However, the destructive and negative tendencies have overstepped the limits of the permissible and as a result young people find themselves victims of the past and hostages to the ongoing reforms. Their innovatory potential has not been claimed by society and their reproductive function is not being realised.

(i)   The *material position* of young people continues to worsen; today two-thirds of them (primarily students and young villagers) live below the official poverty line. We are witnessing a process of impoverishment of youth. The wages of young people, which usually comprise about half of what experienced workers obtain, are continuing to decrease. The housing problem has become even more aggravated: with privatisation, an absolute majority of young people are losing all opportunities for improving their housing conditions. The great material dependence of young people on their parents (80 per cent of young people receive help from their parents) continues to grow. Young people are being squeezed out of the labour market. Mounting unemployment is striking them hard. Approximately one million young people neither work nor study.   Officially about 100,000 persons are registered as being unemployed; yet there is also disguised unemployment which multiplies this number manifold. We are seeing the privatisation of large state enterprises and consequently awaiting an avalanche of unemployment. The social security programme for young people, work on which began in the late 1980s, now stands paralysed.

(ii) *Desocialisation or marginalization* is expanding and deepening. This means that the number of children, teenagers and young people who have become social outcasts is increasing. For different reasons, today the marginals include hopeless young drug addicts (about 500,000), alcoholics, people suffering from particular diseases, 'professional' beggars and tramps (the number of homeless people in Russia is more than a million) and a great number of young invalids (over 1.5 million). They also include young people who have served prison sentences and who wish to be socially useful citizens, but cannot because of the existing social conditions. The number of homeless children, young drug addicts and alcoholics, and under-age unmarried mothers, is rapidly increasing.

The process of youth marginalization is extremely dangerous since it affects the deep layers of consciousness of a substantial number of young people, which may in future seriously affect society in general. In conditions where 60 per cent of the population of Russia consider themselves to be poor, we are witnessing a shift in consciousness and mass psychology towards 'weakness', 'helplessness' and, consequently, to social passivity of millions of people. The problem of an unsettled country, of frustration and disappointment over life's opportunities, over professional and cultural growth, is confronting rural youth particularly strongly. Young people are being obliged to leave their villages and flee to the city in search of work. They are thus breaking all connections with their 'roots'. Very often they fail to find their place in the city and become a sort of 'lumpen proletariat'.

Crisis in the economy and the family, ethnic conflicts and other adverse social processes permit us to assert that the number of marginals in Russia will continue to increase. The 'habitat' of the marginals, which used to be localised, will change its direction and turn towards the central and southern regions of Russia. An analysis of the prospects of growth for each marginal group indicates that the number of homeless people will grow particularly swiftly. In so far as marginalization is closely connected with a decline in living standards, opportunities to receive an education and professional qualifications, Russia can expect the appearance of an entire generation of people who possess neither knowledge nor skills, nor the desire to work in general in the future, a generation of outcasts, of forgotten and lost people.

(iii) *Criminalization of the younger generation* is advancing at a growing rate. Every successive generation of youth is more criminal than the one before. At present, 57 per cent of all crimes are committed by young people. Juvenile crime is growing 15 times more quickly than the general crime rate; so the already enormous criminal potential accumulated in society through the years of totalitarianism and repression (in the last thirty years alone, millions of Soviet citizens passed through prisons and labour camps), continues to grow. This growth is encouraged mainly by the sharply deteriorating socio-economic conditions, the psychological situation, where everything is breaking up, by the demise of former ideals and moral principles (which previously served as a stabilising factor) and by the difficulty of orienting young people on new and unfathomed ideals.

A conflict situation in society is imminent and this is provoking a growth in extremism, aggression and violence. In conditions of chaos, numerous loop-holes for criminal activity appear. The flow of refugees, who travel from place to place without financial support and legal protection, insecurity and family conflict, the fall in the prestige of education and culture are leading to a cult of power. The increase in juvenile crime causes enormous material and moral damage to society in general and to the young people themselves. Today, the concept of youth is associated with the concept of cruelty, violence and danger. Adults begin to fear and hate teenagers.

According to specialist forecasts, juvenile crime will continue to grow. Robberies, thefts, racketeering and speculation will spread more widely. The number of juveniles drawn into the selling of drugs, gambling, prostitution and misappropriation of arms, will increase. Crime will start to decrease only when the socio-economic, political and moral situation in society drastically improves and when the state pursues effective social policies geared towards youth, one of the directions of which should be to combat juvenile crime.

(iv) *Deteriorating economic crisis will lead to a further worsening of the social position of young people.* The circumstances of youth will depend on a continuation of the aforementioned tendencies: declining employment and growing unemployment, falling incomes and personal consumption expenditure, increasing deviant behaviour and crime, the serious aggravation of many problems in the spheres of public health, intellectual, spiritual and moral development and leisure time. The position of young people cannot be improved if we attempt to resolve it outside the context of the general issues facing Russian society. The present crisis is not of a temporary character, it reflects past, present and future tendencies. That is why these problems can be solved only within the general Russian context on a long-term basis with full recognition of the interconnection and inter-dependence existing between economic and political reforms and social policy.

Political status

Perestroika was a shock to the *political consciousness* of young people. It ardently supported the fairly restrained (at least on current standards) ideas for transforming society. Young people made up the mass of participants in democratic demonstrations, meetings, strikes and national-patriotic manifestations. The 'new political thinking' spread widely within the youth movement and young people became an active factor in socio-political change.

However, the economic crisis, which followed soon after perestroika, the progressive deterioration of the material situation and the public's conditions of life and the mistakes made in implementing economic reform, all provoked frustration and political apathy among young people. As a result, they turned away from politics. To a large extent, this was a reaction to official indifference to the lives of young people, to their inability to carry through a serious youth policy. The main concern of the absolute majority of young people today is to struggle for survival. They are worried how and where they will be able to earn something in order to buy food and clothes. What is more, they can rely only on themselves and on their relatives. We are observing today the atomisation and disintegration of society. Growing unemployment condemns young people to competition in the labour market, including competition among their peers. The existing political parties, youth organisations, trade unions and most politicians, for various reasons, do not enjoy the confidence of the young.

The anticipated upheaval in the youth movement failed to materialise; new youth organisations do not have a developed organisational structure, neither do they have a solid material and financial base. These organisations are few in number and their weight in 'big politics' and their influence on young people are minimal. Young people are used by diminutive parties in their own interests but they are at loggerheads with each other. In other words, *the subjectivity of young people, and consequently, their role in social life, politics and protection of their own interests has not grown; on the contrary, it has fallen even more.* In fact, young people, with all their problems, have been left to the mercy of fate and they find themselves in the position of victims of political, separatist and nationalistic ambitions. As before, they are not allowed to enter into the structure of power. The number of young people working in representative bodies of power has diminished three-fold over the last ten years. There is only one person under 30 in the Russian parliament.

Russia can emerge from the period of crisis and social catastrophe only by enhancing the role of politics in the life of the society, at least in the initial stage of reform. *A change of political generations is unavoidable, and it is already taking place. Politicians who have already exhausted their potential and have become 'outdated' are disappearing into the background. They are being replaced by new political leaders with their own 'teams'.*

New generations of politicians will emerge from the youth environment and this presupposes that young people will participate in politics; for that to happen they will have to study politics from the early years and cultivate a taste for it. Russian society should advocate the idea of *politization of public life* in order to apply a strong social pressure on the authorities in favour of reforms, through parties, political movements and organisations, including youth associations. Any shunning of politics means acquiescing to the powers that be, which engenders arbitrary rule, and, in the long-run, tyranny. *The drawing of young people into politics is imperative for the present and the future.*

Young people's *interest* in politics is considerable. For example, in February 1993, young people answered the question 'Do you take an interest in politics?' as follows: great interest, 15.4 per cent; some interest 57.7 per cent and no interest in politics 26.9 per cent. In the long-term, if the socio-economic and material position of youth continues to deteriorate, political curiosity and interest will turn into political activity leading to young people taking part in mass movements for their rights. The situation in the youth environment is explosive as never before. Social problems today affect all groups of young people: schoolchildren, students, young workers and farmers, engineers and technicians, soldiers and officers. They may well renounce their traditional role of a force that is led and become an active *participant* in social conflict and change by taking a leading role, thereby becoming the main spokesperson for people's frustrated hopes, for people's anxieties and for people's wrath. The aggravation of young people's social problems has led to a situation where the moods of social protest are accumulating more and more. In our survey of February 1993, only 16.4 per cent of those interviewed said 'No' to the question: 'Are young people likely to take action against the authorities?'. Over 21 per cent of the 1,037 young people interviewed felt that a social explosion was possible; 11.8 per cent said it was inevitable and 19.2 per cent stated they were ready to take part in such actions.

Moods, values and orientations

The deterioration of the youth economic and social position has led to a *worsening mood and psychological atmosphere among young people.* Psychological studies show that a substantial proportion of young people lack independence and confidence in themselves. They are a highly volatile group and the level of their social activity is extremely low. Their social mood can best be described as one of 'disappointment', 'pessimism', 'hopelessness', 'confusion', 'apathy', 'aggression', 'anger' and/or 'extremism'. Surveys also show that young people are experiencing fear and considerable fear at that. For many young people, life has lost its meaning: the number of suicides is increasing. In the future, this tendency will probably grow, particularly when unemployment becomes more widespread.

The youth of Russia, like society as a whole, is undergoing a crisis of values. The demise of totalitarianism brought with it the destruction of former ideals and values ('communism', 'Marxism-Leninism', 'socialism', 'revolution', 'class', 'class struggle', 'proletarian internationalism', 'Communist Party', 'Young Communist League' etc.), which were part of people's inner world. The superficially easy renouncement of traditional values for many people turned into a painful re-assessment of these values. Although they lost all practical meaning and took on a negative connotation, the old values did not disappear from popular consciousness. New values ('freedom', 'democracy', 'market economy', 'equal opportunities', 'private property', 'the rule of law'), are as yet incomprehensible, and many people have not accepted them because, in their practical meaning, they are mostly associated with negative phenomena, negative feelings and sensations ('democracy' equals corruption; 'market' means poverty etc.). In the popular consciousness, and particularly in individual consciousness, a *spiritual vacuum* has formed.

The driving out of old values and the assimilation of new ones will take quite a long time even for those young people who are capable of self-development and intensive work of the soul and intellect. We are concerned about the *spiritual-moral marginalization* of young people; there is likely to be a further growth in soullessness and immorality, until marked changes for the better appear in socio-economic and political life; in other words, until the values of society are changed in a positive direction.

The following tendencies can be observed in the world of youth values in the period 1992-94:

(i)   practically all young people (approximately 97 per cent) show a negative attitude to communism and socialism as values. At the same time, the concepts 'equality', 'fraternity', 'justice', 'collectivism', 'internationalism', 'combined personal and social interests' - the essence of socialism - engage the consciousness of a substantial proportion of young people (up to 50 per cent); the significance of these concepts continues to grow;

(ii) political values lie on the periphery of the value system of young people. However, youth political consciousness is of a pendulum character: it swings from one extreme under the impact of events and then to the other under the influence of other events;

(iii) the youth value orientation is affected by the rapid growth of national and nationalistic factors. We note the growth of 'wounded' national self-awareness among Russian youth. Chauvinistic moods are becoming stronger;

(iv) the structure of youth consciousness shows an increase in universal humanitarian values: health, family, love etc., and of individual values, such as personal success, material security and comfort;

(v) the law is being valued less and less. A substantial proportion of young people see nothing reprehensible in breaking the law; what is more, many youngsters consider it to be inevitable;

(vi) the value of religion and the church has notably grown. An irrationalization of the spiritual world is taking place and young people are becoming more predisposed to mysticism; and

(vii) the economic factor strongly affects youth value orientations: the lower the level of their material well-being, the more evident is their aspiration for a 'strong hand'. In some young people, the basis for fascism has already formed.

In the main, the analysis of the youth system demonstrates that some youngsters *have already passed the lowest point of the shock stage*, the state of disappointment, confusion and lack of belief. Some young people have found spiritual and moral support in freedom and democracy, as supreme values of the new society. They see the meaning of their life in the simultaneous satisfaction of their individual needs and in such suprapersonal values as the *narod* (people), Motherland, science, art etc. This section among the young, as in 'adult' society, is very small for the moment, yet it does exist and will continue to grow. It is very important that this section has appeared and there must be conditions for its further growth, in as much as this is the *leading section* of society which exerts a determining influence on its life. In the coming years, there is likely to be a sharp intensification of commercialization, materialization, rationalization and competition in youth consciousness. This development will widen the gap between material and spiritual orientations. Vulgar materialism will repress the spiritual principles of life, thus destroying the fundamentals of its own development.   The humanization of education must counterbalance this tendency and help prevent any further deformation of young people's spiritual and moral world, otherwise Russian society will not quickly and easily recover from the present spiritual and moral crisis. The moulding of the 'new' individual with the help of a powerful system of education and the repression of all dissent by violent means went on for some 80 years, throughout the lifetime of nearly three generations. A new generation can *grow up* only with the replacement of generations, each of which will shed the load of those ideas, views and values which impede progress. However, this will take time and cannot be achieved within the life-span of a single generation.

General conclusions

This study shows that *every successive generation of young people of Russia is, according to its social position and development, worse off than the one before it.*   It is less healthy and less developed mentally, less spiritual and less cultured, but more immoral and more criminal. Its attitude to work is becoming increasingly poor, it manifests a growing alienation from knowledge and education, from politics, society and the state. What kind of future awaits Russia with its younger generation? The relationship between the concepts 'youth' and 'the future', 'social development of society' and 'the development of young people' is obvious. Social processes are not mechanical or automatic in nature, they are changeable, and different versions of development are possible.

I would like to end by considering two possible future directions regarding the status and development of youth in post-Soviet society.

(i)   The pessimistic scenario

If an end is not put to the negative processes and tendencies in the youth environment, if the course of events is not changed, they will become irreversible and Russia will be in for a global social catastrophe. Russia naturally has a future even in the worst scenario.   It will continue to exist even if the nation breaks up into many parts.   One such part will be called Russia.   But the great, proud and powerful

Russia will be no more. It will be a geographically small entity with significant resources of raw materials. Its population will not be large, and its people will be unhealthy and poorly developed, both physically and mentally. It will be a Russia with poor economic, intellectual and cultural potential. It will be a weak and dependent country with a superiority complex about the past and an inferiority complex about the present. If one looks at things honestly, such a picture of the future is quite probable. If we seriously examine the processes taking place in the younger generation, we cannot call them progressive, they cannot be termed 'development'. It is change, but change for the worse. It is not progress, it is regress. If we agree that this regress has been going on for many decades, we can come to only one conclusion that the Russian nation is degrading, degenerating and slowly perishing. This tragic summary goes against the proud Russian spirit for it is insulating and offensive, it sounds like a condemnation. This conclusion is not perceived by the ordinary consciousness because social processes proceed latently and unhurriedly, they stretch over decades and centuries and are, therefore, inconspicuous. However, facts and figures do not allow any other interpretation of the situation. Moreover, this conclusion should be worded more strongly, for the circumstances of the last few years have strengthened, accelerated and aggravated all the existing negative processes, lending them a catastrophic character. New tendencies have appeared and their scope is rapidly expanding. These tendencies are marginalization, forced migration, nationalism, religious fundamentalism and so forth. All this means that society should not set too much store by youth as the hope and 'support' of the reforms. The creative, innovatory potential of the young (health, intellectual development, quality of knowledge and of professional training, attitudes to work, level of social activity, value orientations etc.) does not correspond to those complex problems which have to be resolved in the course of the transformation of totalitarian society.

(ii) An optimistic scenario

It is important to recognise that the problems mentioned herein are the result of tendencies which originated long ago. Life has become difficult for society and the young not because reforms have been launched. The reforms exposed all the bad things and gave us the opportunity to understand how badly matters stand. Negative tendencies have an accumulative character. These tendencies have turned into 'negative' laws of Russian society, laws which do not 'work' either for development or for progress. On the contrary, these laws 'work' against them, they 'work' for the destruction of the Russian nation and the Russian people.

The social status and level of development of Russian youth in contemporary society depends mainly on those cardinal changes in its socio-economic and political structure which have occurred in the last eight years. The historical moment in which we live today represents a transitional period from one socio-political system (totalitarianism) to an entirely different, opposite social structure in which the entire system of values is ruled by freedom. In this respect, the existing situation is a temporary one. It is only natural that the transitional period should be accompanied by much necessary and inevitable destructive work, the consequences of which are none the less inevitable, negative processes.

In the youth environment, as in society in general, we observe today the prevalence of destructive over creative activities, and positive changes. Such a situation is the result of impotence by the authorities at all levels to carry out an organic evolutionary development of the reforms, which precludes extreme measures. It is located somewhere between the two extreme positions - e.g. the optimum; to find it requires considerable knowledge, creative talent and intuition. It is obvious that present-day politicians, including the top figures, lack these qualities. It is also obvious that (i) all ideas of a quick recovery from the crisis are nothing but political adventurism; (ii) the nation's improvement can be brought about only through the improvement and development of several generations of young people, and (iii) socio-economic reforms (owing to the first two circumstances) and all their specific programmes should deliberately be oriented on the future, and be associated with youth who should be not only the subject of education and training, but a *conscious participant* in social transformation.

The leading and determining idea of Russian reforms and development should not merely be the 'new economic order' and 'market economy' by themselves, taken out of context, but human beings themselves who understand the meaning of the reforms and who actively participate in them. The main characteristic of political thinking today must be comprehension of the new role of the human factor in development. *The main form of accumulation of public wealth is identified with the accumulation not of things and finance capital, but mainly of new knowledge and other useful information, the bearers of which are the people.* The direction, content and character of the historical process now depends not so much on the material factors as on the will (both individually and collectively), on the reaction of this will and intellect in the emergent problems of socio-political life. The difficulty here lies not in the reiteration of this postulate, but in actually recognising human beings as the principal figures in the philosophy of Russian development, in building up the ideology of reform, invariably proceeding from this fulcrum. In the long-run, the solution of all the problems of social development depends upon the formation in Russia of a culture of a new time; this would include a renewed understanding of life, a renewed system of spiritual and moral values. In order to change nature and society, people themselves must change in the course of implementing humanistic reform oriented on the future and the future generation.

Not merely human beings but *young people as bearers of the future, the source of innovation and of change* should become the focus of contemporary politics. Above all, young people today represent the main sphere of contemporary financial, material and spiritual investment. Russia cannot permit itself a policy aimed at gaining immediate benefits without giving thought to the consequences for any action or measures it takes. Russia should invest in the young, for in this way it invests in its own future (see Chapter 13). The time has come when we should speak of the new discovery of youth, it is time we understood that youth is the most fruitful period of a person's lifetime, it is a period when he or she more than ever before aspires to self-assertion and self-realization. Youth represents a value of a special order, it is the prime value of society. Youth is not only a demographic concept, it is also an economic, social and political one.

Such an approach to the assessment of the young and investment in future generations will enable us to elaborate such a policy by state and society, which will make it possible to control the processes and move ahead of events. This policy should replace the one we are following today, a policy which shows a retarded reaction to contradictions and problems that have already emerged. This new policy will make it possible to accelerate the development of the country and support its *breakthrough* to the front line of social progress.

Notes

The references in this chapter are mainly taken from research collected from a number of youth research sources and not previously published in book or article form. This was common practice in Soviet times: such information gathering provided the authorities, particularly the Young Communist League (Komsomol), with some insight into what young people were thinking and doing. But the information was not available for general circulation.

These 'public opinion' surveys' were largely organised from Moscow by the Research Centre attached to the Youth Institute (previously the Higher Komsomol School); the Centre's chief for several years was this chapter's author, Professor Igor Ilynsky. Material was also sent to this Centre by the Population Centre of the Lomonosov Moscow State University, the Socio-Economic Population Institute of the Russian Academy of Sciences, the Comprehensive Social Research Institute attached to Saint Petersburg University, the Socio-Political Research Institute of the Russian Academy of Sciences, the Labour Institute attached to the Russian Federation Ministry of Labour, the Russian Management Academy, and the Research Institute for the Health and Therapy of Children, Teenagers and Young Adults.

See also I.M. Ilynsky and A.V. Sharonov (eds), *Molodyozh Rossii. Tendentsii, Perspektivy* (Moscow, Nauchno-issledovatelsky tsentr pri Institut molodyozhi, 1993).

2 'Respectable fears' versus 'moral panics': Youth as a social problem in Russia and Britain

CHRISTOPHER WILLIAMS

Introduction

The purpose of this chapter is to compare and contrast official attitudes towards youth in Russia and Britain. The key question addressed is the extent to which 'youth' is considered a 'social problem'. Youth attitudes towards drinking, smoking, drug abuse, sex and crime are examined. But before we can proceed, a number of conceptual and methodological issues must be outlined.

Conceptual and methodological problems

It is necessary, first of all, to define what we consider to be 'youth'. In Britain, the term 'youth' normally refers to teenagers. However, in Russian terminology according to Jim Riordan, 'youth' refers to those aged between 15-30 years.[1] In order to try and simplify the following discussion, I will largely confine my discussion to the notion of 'teenager' (i.e. those between 13-19 years) when referring to 'youth' in this chapter.

The second conceptual issue relates to what we mean by 'social problem'. Following Timms,[2] a social problem can be defined as social behaviour (drinking, smoking, crime etc.) that causes public friction and/or private misery. However, the question of who says a given activity constitutes a social problem and why, is itself a highly subjective issue. Thus powerful groups in either Russia and/or Britain may be in a position to describe the behaviour of individuals or groups as a threat to their own or national interests. To take an example, young people in any society may be labelled 'trouble-makers' by certain authority groups ranging from police officers through to psychiatrists in the case of Britain and by the militsia, Komsomol and the medical profession in the former Soviet Union (hereafter FSU).

This brings us to another aspect of this question, namely how is a particular problem formulated and whose version is to be believed? The answer to such questions centres on the status of those involved, their access to the policy and decision-making process as well as the mass media and other institutions through which their version of events could be amplified and made more credible by their status. This allows professionals to render alternative versions of events invalid by a process of labelling certain categories of youth as 'mentally deficient'; 'criminal' etc.

Following on from this discussion, there is the fourth aspect relating to what (and whose) theories are used to explain the problem or perhaps more accurately to explain it away? These questions point to the inter-relationship between social and sociological problems in both countries discussed in this chapter. Hence some facet of social behaviour - say crime - conducted by one particular group - youth - may be perceived as a 'social problem' and explained in terms of sociological theory and analysis. While my intention is not to explain away youth crime as a major issue in Russia and Britain since the 1950s, it must nevertheless be emphasised that the nature of this problem may have been exaggerated because the theories used are those emanating from those in control positions who are able to act upon their own theories e.g. police, courts etc. In this sense, therefore, theories about youth behaviour in general or crime in particular are not only about the problem at hand but also a part of it. Thus the law is determined by those with the power and the authority, for instance the former nomenklatura elites in the ex-Communist Party of the Soviet Union (or CPSU).

In the context of the subject of this chapter, there is an additional unresolved problem, namely: how far do professional theories or government attitudes amplify the nature of the problem? With regard to juvenile delinquency, there are possibly two forms of deviancy amplification. The first refers to the so-called ICEBERG effect which means that research into the characteristics of youths who misbehave provides a checklist of pointers for various professional groups - teachers, psychiatrists, lawyers, policemen etc. - who then use these features to discover new cases thereby enabling juvenile delinquency to be viewed as a serious problem. Cohen suggested this was the case with 'Mods and Rockers' in the UK in the 1950s and 1960s.[3] Thus if the general public perceives a 'crime wave', owing to mass media sensationalism, then there will be a tendency for more crime to be reported, so more of the iceberg will appear above the surface. The second problem involved relates to the so-called REACTION effect. If those working in juvenile detention centres or prisons theorise that inmates are 'wicked' and 'badly socialised' individuals and then act upon these beliefs, it is highly probable that they will look for (and hence perhaps find) evidence reinforcing such in-built prejudices. If we are not careful, therefore, social science disciplines, such as sociology, can be used to produce a self *fulfilling prophecy* in the sense that they can be used to define 'youth' as a problem for society. While such theories can be useful in explaining particular 'social problems', we must be aware that identifying a certain act (drug use) or group (youth) as a social problem necessitates passing a value judgement upon both. It was this concern that prompted me to contrast respectable fears and moral panics. This dilemma must be borne in mind throughout the following discussion.

Risk Takers:[4] Drinking, smoking, drugs and sex among youth in Russia and Britain

This section looks at potential areas of young people's behaviour which might be considered a 'social problem' in both societies before turning to discuss the question of juvenile delinquency in greater depth in the second half of this chapter. Drinking and smoking habits will be considered first, before we turn to analyse drug abuse and sexual behaviour among young people. Each country will be examined separately and in the process differences and similarities in trends and approaches will be highlighted.

Drinking habits among youth

It is useful at the outset to provide some indication of alcohol consumption trends in Russia and Britain. In 1988, the situation was as shown in Table 2.1 below which shows considerable national variations in alcohol consumption in both countries. The problem is that this Table takes beer, wine and spirits together in order to reach the figures stated. This means that although Russia appears to possess lower per capita alcohol consumption than the UK by 1988, in actual fact such a statement is misleading because there are different traditions of drinking in each country, with Russians consuming more spirits and those from Britain more beer:

Table 2.1
Alcohol consumption in UK and ex-USSR, 1970-88
(litres per capita of 100% alcohol)

Countries	*Year and alcohol consumption*				
	1970	*1975*	*1980*	*1985*	*1988*
UK	5.3	6.8	7.2	7.2	7.4
ex-USSR	6.8	6.8	8.8	7.2	3.6

Source: M. Plant and M. Plant, *Risk Takers: Alcohol, Drugs, Sex and Youth* (Routledge, London, 1992), pp. 14-15.

Russia

In Soviet and now post-Communist Russia, heavy drinking was one of the most deep rooted traditions.[5] Successive leaderships in the FSU have been concerned about the negative impact of alcoholism on economic performance, mortality patterns, traffic and industrial accidents, crime and domestic violence which led to divorce.[6]

Drinking among young people was considered a very serious issue. Official concern stemmed from the fact that some parents in Russia encouraged their children to drink at an early age.[7] Surveys of Soviet youth in the Communist period reveal that children in Russia first tasted alcohol at the average age of 11.5 years.[8] As regards alcohol consumption trends, when Nagaev investigated the situation in Perm in 1971, he discovered that of 2,027 people surveyed, 82 per cent in the age group 16-18 years consumed alcohol and, of this group, 20.5 per cent of males and 13.8 per cent of females systematically purchased alcohol; similarly when Levin questioned older school children in 1972, he discovered that 75 per cent of boys and 40 per cent of girls aged 15 had tried alcohol, as had 80 per cent and 60 per cent respectively at 16 and 95 per cent of boys and 90 per cent of girls at the age of 17. Of this sample, 17 per cent of boys and 10 per cent of girls stated that they had started to drink at the age of 13-14 years; 35 per cent and 38 per cent respectively began at 15-16 and 27 per cent of boys and 42 per cent of girls started drinking between the ages of 17-19 years.[9] Soviet research also ascertained that attitudes towards alcohol within the family unit determine children's beliefs on drinking,[10] as does the influence of peer groups and work mates in the case of working juveniles. Other scholars expressed great concern about the indifference of teachers, employers, Komsomol and party organisations to juvenile drinking.[11]

Obviously, much has changed since the late 1960s to mid-1970s, but the 1980s saw a continuation of these earlier trends and led to the introduction of an anti-alcohol campaign under Gorbachev.[12] Unfortunately, the latter was only partly successful because fiscal concerns outweighed other factors. As a result, drinking among post-Communist youth continues to be widespread.

Britain

Drinking in Britain is viewed as a legitimate and enjoyable activity, with the Plants' arguing that the UK has a 'wet' culture.[13] Surveys carried out throughout Scotland and England show that most 10-14 year olds have consumed alcohol. For example, 80 per cent of 13 year old males and 74 per cent of females drank alcohol in England and Wales compared to 68 per cent of males and 54 per cent of females in Scotland. However, by the age of 17, this gap had narrowed significantly, as had the tendency to consume alcohol. Thus 91 per cent of 17 year old males and 88 per cent of females in England and Wales compared to 86 per cent of males and 89 per cent of females in Scotland drank alcohol by the mid-1980s.[14] Not only do teenagers in the UK tend to favour alcohol and become aware of alcohol at an early age, many also wished that the legal drinking age be reduced from 18 to 16 years.[15]   However, it is the 'misuse' of alcohol by teenagers which has become the focus of public concern.   This debate has centred on the impact which heavy drinking has on mortality, accidents at work or on the roads (in the latter case 10 per cent of 16-19 year olds were killed in 1988)[16] or on the crime rate.   For instance, in England and Wales in 1989, 3,357 males and 416 females under 18 years were found guilty or cautioned for offences relating to drunkenness.[17]   As a consequence, Martin and Moira Plant conclude that 'alcohol misuse amongst young people has become established as a chronic problem in the United Kingdom'.[18]

Smoking among youth

Russia

The tendency for a large number of people from Russia to smoke has generated alarm.[19]   Although it is widely known that young people in Russia smoke cigarettes, exact data are difficult to obtain.   However, one survey carried out in 25 key towns of the USSR in the early 1970s discovered that 18.2 per cent of males and 1.5 per cent of females aged between 16-19 years smoked.[20]   As with alcohol earlier, the main motives were imitation (*podrazhanie*) of peer groups, friends or simply the desire to be fashionable; curiosity (*liubopytstvo*); addiction to nicotine; the wish to diet or the desire to appear grown up.[21]   Smoking in Russia is a contributory factor to the emergence of heart disease, cancer and various respiratory diseases. Although young people in Russia are aware of the dangers of smoking, many teenagers still smoke.   Despite official concerns about mortality increases, especially among males, successive leaderships in Russia were slow to embark upon anti-smoking campaigns.   The 'fiscal dilemma' was largely responsible.   As the market economy takes hold in the mid-late 1990s, the smoke ring - the tie between government and big business - in Russia will get stronger and stronger with the consequence that the aforementioned health problems, not yet readily apparent among Russian teenagers, will take their toll later in middle age.

Britain

Like alcohol earlier, smoking too is also common among British teenagers. However, smoking as a trend is on the decline. Thus Foster *et al.* discovered that the proportion of males aged 16-19 years who smoked fell from 43 per cent in 1972 to 28 per cent in 1988. The corresponding figures for females were 39 to 28 per cent.[22] As a consequence of the campaigns launched by ASH (Action on Smoking and Health), the dangers of smoking are now widely known (i.e. that tobacco smoking is implicated in approximately a third of cancer and 90 per cent of lung cancer deaths in Britain).[23] However, this has not stopped teenagers taking up the habit. Goddard's 1990 study of 11-19 year olds in various secondary schools throughout England and Wales found, for example, that having brothers and sisters or parents who smoked was highly influential, as was a tolerant attitude towards smoking, peer pressure and so forth.[24] UK surveys have also found large regional variations in smoking patterns. For instance, although smoking has declined in the UK throughout the 1980s, this fall has not been so marked in Scotland and the north of England.[25]

According to Taylor, it is the 'smoke ring' (i.e. the ring of political and economic interests protecting the tobacco industry) which is to blame for the overall lack of action on smoking in Britain. As he puts it: 'The main reason why governments have taken so little action against the product (tobacco), which has been responsible for the deaths of millions of its citizens is because governments are themselves part of the Smoke Ring'.[26] Thus instead of protecting adults and teenagers from the negative impact of smoking, the British government actively promotes tobacco for fear of increasing unemployment and losing trade, on the one hand, and because it is dependent on the revenues which it gets from tobacco, on the other.[27] We saw above that a similar situation prevails in Russia.

Drug use as a youth problem

While widespread drinking and smoking among teenagers in Russia and Britain has been the focus of official concern in both countries since the 1960s, this has partly been replaced from the 1970s onwards with governmental as well as public concern regarding the use of illicit drugs.

The definition of 'illicit drugs' varies according to which society and culture we are referring to. Thus in the case of Britain, under the parameters laid down by the 1971 Misuse of Drugs Act, cocaine, opium, heroin, methadone, morphine, LSD, mescaline, psilocybin, cannabis, amphetamines, 'angel dust' and a variety of tranquillisers are all viewed as illicit drugs.[28]   Similar debates have taken place in Russia since the 1920s and 1930s.[29]

Russia

An analysis of drug problems in Russia is essential because it is seen as a problem amongst youth.

The number of drug addicts in Russia is difficult to estimate firstly because of the many imprecise definitions used to describe the nature of the problem, such as abuse; addiction; dependency; misuse etc. and secondly because Russia has only published even incomplete data since 1988.[30]   However, the number of officially registered 'drug addicts' and 'toxic substance abusers' increased from 2.5 per 100,000 population in 1985 to 4.8 per 100,000 by 1989.[31]   Izvestiia argues more specifically that of the 52,000 registered drug addicts in 1988, individuals under 30, including 14,000 minors, made up 62 per cent of the total.   Furthermore, of the 22,000 toxic substance abusers, 13,000 were minors.[32]

Since the collapse of the USSR in late 1991, the full extent of the problem has emerged. By 1991, there were 1.5m drug users in Russia alone, but two years later this total had risen to between 5.5-7.5m.[33]   A powerful drug mafia has now emerged, making the task of combating the drugs problem extremely difficult. In the communist phase, an increasing number of drug users were referred to medical establishments for treatment, with the proportion rising from 13.7 per 100,000 in 1985 to 27.1 per 100,000 by 1987.   However, drug rehabilitation and education programmes, especially among youth, were poorly organised. The collapse of the Union in 1991 hampered the development of a more integrated approach to the problem.

In the past, militia crackdowns were used to confiscate supplies and jail pushers. But in early 1992, the Russian Criminal Code was amended so that it was no longer a crime to be in possession of drugs for personal use.[34] While this move away from earlier victim-blaming approach is to be welcomed, it has not been accompanied by the introduction of widespread and effective anti-drug propaganda among teenagers or the creation of large numbers of drug treatment centres.[35]   In the long-term, therefore, neutral, indifferent attitudes towards the problem, especially in traditional drug trafficking routes in Central Asia, but also in the new transfer routes in the Baltics, Ukraine and Belarus, increase the likelihood of more young drug abusers in the future.

Britain

Although drug taking in Britain has been established since the early part of this century, with a Dangerous Drugs Act made law in 1920, it was not until the 1960s and 1970s, alongside dress - mini skirts, and music - the Beatles and the Rolling Stones - that drug use, especially of cannabis, became associated with the emerging youth culture.   A series of studies have all discovered that teenagers and students often use drugs.   For example, Swadi's 1988 survey of 3,333 London comprehensive school children found that one in five of those aged 11-16 had used illicit drugs or solvents, with 8 per cent repeatedly using drugs and 5.8 per cent using LSD, cocaine, heroin or tranquillisers.[36]   The number of narcotic addicts known to the authorities (i.e. based on Home Office data) has increased from 1,426 (of which 73.7 per cent were male and 26.3 per cent female) in 1970 to 17,755 (of which 72.1 per cent were male and 27.9 per cent female) in 1990.   In this 20 year period, the number of known addicts has therefore increased nearly thirteen-fold.[37]   In 1989, 954 males and 489 females under 21 years were classified as drug addicts.   In the same year, 38,415 persons were found guilty of drug offences.   Of the latter group, 33,669 had used cannabis, 2,395 am-phetamines and 1,769 heroin.   The rest used a variety of other drugs, such as cocaine, LSD etc.[38]   Many addicts, of course, have died as a result of their addictions.   For example, 1,499 'notified addicts' in the UK died in the period 1967-81 alone.   Since then the total has been steadily rising.   For instance, a total of 1,200 people died of drugs-related causes in 1989.[39]

Sexual attitudes among youth

This topic is viewed by most as central to any understanding of 'youth' in the late twentieth century.   For instance, Moore and Rosenthal argue that: 'All theories of adolescent development give sexuality a central place in negotiating the transition from child to adult'[40] while Griffin adds 'Adolescence as a concept is distinctly sexualized'.[41]

Russia

In Russia, Kon and Riordan as well as Williams found that despite puritanical attitudes towards sex in Russia from Stalin to Gorbachov, a liberal attitude prevailed among Soviet youth.[42] As a result, many Russians begin their sex lives early. Thus 10.3 per cent of boys and 17 per cent of girls began an active sex life before the age of 16 years whereas 75 per cent of men and 63.3 per cent of women began having sex between the ages of 16-21.[43] Unfortunately there is a long established tradition of ignorance of sex in Russia and a low contraceptive culture. Despite AIDS,[44] attitudinal changes have been difficult to achieve because Russia has a long tradition of sexual taboos and so in the pre-Gorbachov period, successive governments refused to patronise disciplines central to sex education, such as *seksologiia*. This lack of a sexual culture has had a deleterious effect on youth who are sexually backward, unhappy and suffering from serious neuroses about sex. The explosion of sexual literature in books, newspapers, such as *Sobesednik, SPID-info* etc., since the late 1980s has, according to Kon, generated a moral panic of the type talked of by Cohen several decades ago.[45] As Attwood comments 'Suddenly the image of the enthusiastic clean-cut Young Communist marching purposefully along the golden road to Communism was replaced by that of the unkempt, amoral cynic, as much into sex and drugs and rock and roll as his - or her - Western counterpart'.[46] Films such as *Malenkaia Vera* (1988), *Tragediia v stile rok* (1988) or *Ch P raionnovo masshtaba* (1989) epitomise such a view of ex-Soviet youth. The Soviet and post-Communist regimes were, of course, unprepared for this and responded in the time honoured tradition by viewing Russian youth like its British counterpart as a social problem for society, as such Western habits marked, according to Soviet experts, a 'decline in ideological commitment'.[47]

Britain

The trend since the 1960s has been towards the first experience of sex at a younger age. Ford and Morgan note, for example, that of a sample of 17 year old British adolescents, 63 per cent said they were 'sexually experienced'; 40 per cent reported that their sexual debut took place at 15 years and a further 9 per cent stated that their first sexual experience was at 13 years or younger. Another study discovered that half its respondents had had sex before the age of 18 years and 75 per cent had done so before the age of twenty.[48] However, the advent of AIDS has perhaps changed attitudes. Moore and Rosenthal suggest that there was a considerable increase in condom use among adolescents in the 1980s, with the use of this contraceptive doubling for boys and girls.[49] However, a note of caution must also be sounded. A series of studies have investigated the level of knowledge of HIV and AIDS among young people throughout the UK. They demonstrate some confusion on the part of youth. Thus of one group aged 18-21 years in a Scottish survey covering the period 1988-1992, 21.9 per cent viewed donating blood; 17.9 per cent wet kissing; 4.9 per cent use of public toilets and 3.6 per cent eating food prepared by AIDS patients as possible sources of infection.[50]

On the basis of the above evidence, many argue that young people pose a danger to themselves. This view focuses on what is seen as excessive behaviour among youth. Thus young people drink and smoke too much, experiment with drugs and engage in unsafe or dangerous sexual behaviour. It is not surprising then that adolescent behaviour in general is viewed as deviant. Hence they are either viewed as risk-takers[51] or as adventurers.[52] This negative, and not always accurate image, is compounded by the other lifestyles referred to earlier. The outcome is, as Plant and Plant conclude that '... on balance, available evidence supports the view that there is an association between alcohol, certain other drugs and risky sex (among youth)'.[53]

The way teenagers view themselves, of course, is at odds with official or professional images. One of the ways in which sociologists in particular have tried to examine these opposing images is through the use of the term 'youth culture'.

The Politics of Age: The emergence of a youth culture

We have seen above that the notion of 'youth' is a complex issue and investigating various aspects of youth behaviour - drinking, smoking, drug usage and sexual behaviour - is problematic. Thus far we have examined youth lifestyles through the eyes of officialdom and assumed for the sake of argument that there were certain commonalities between British and Russian youth. However, it is clear that up until 1985, or perhaps more accurately since 1992, Russian and Western youth were the product of different cultural traditions and values. While this important topic cannot be addressed in full here, some appreciation of the notion of 'youth culture' is vital to a clearer understanding of past and current representations of youth.

According to Brake, a youth culture provides young people with an opportunity with which to explore their own identity. This is an identity separate from the roles and expectations imposed upon them by agencies of political socialisation, such as the family and the education system. Furthermore, youth culture offers young people a collective identity and reference point from which they are able to develop their own identities as individuals.[54] More specifically, Frith argues that youth culture is best seen as groups of teenagers who possess some shared activities, values and characteristics in relation to fashion, musical tastes, politics etc.[55] A combination of these two definitions will be assumed in the discussion that follows.

Sociological perspectives on youth culture

Russia

As numerous other scholars, most notably Riordan, Bushnell and Pilkington have already dealt with this question in a Russian context,[56] only brief comments need be made here. During the Communist era, Soviet scholars argued that the New Soviet man/woman was not adversely affected by Western bourgeois culture.[57] However, during the Gorbachev period, 'glasnost' exposed this view as inaccurate.[58] This is shown by the fact that youth in Russia has for decades, but especially since the mid-1980s, embraced and strongly imitated Western youth culture. The extent to which young people throughout Russia should be rejecting their own national youth cultures in favour of an alien Western one is a matter for continued debate between Westerners and Slavophiles in the leaderships of the FSU. As Russia is in flux, it is likely to be some time yet before Russian youth finds its own voice and acts upon it and before dominant Communist discourses on Russian youth are broken down. The same can also be said of Britain in the aftermath of the Thatcher decade.

Britain

In the early stages youth cultures were not viewed as a threat to society[59] but seen, in Britain at least, as part of the evolving mass culture.[60] Elsewhere, however, such as in the United States, two forms of youth culture were said to exist: one which fitted in with American values and was viewed as conformist; the other as symbolised by films such as *Rebel Without a Cause; The Wild Ones* or *The Blackboard Jungle* challenged the establishment and were later associated with the student movements of the 1960s and 1970s - sit-ins, demonstrations, campaigns and protests (e.g. May 1968 in France; the Prague Spring or the politicisation of youth against the Vietnam War in the USA).

In Russia prior to Gorbachev, youth cultures were viewed as a threat to the status-quo and ideological conformity; but since the mid-1980s, some of the so-called *neformal'nye* (informal) youth groups have been tolerated (e.g. rock-music fans; hippies etc.) but others have not (namely hooligans, such as the *liubery*; or extreme nationalists such as *Pamyat*').[61]

Although Western scholars reached the conclusion that most rebellious teenagers later turn out to be 'normal adults',[62] officialdom has become obsessed that many juveniles did not develop into well-balanced, conformist individuals in adulthood. In viewing most of youth in this way, governments and some specialists have helped perpetuate the view that teenagers in Russia and Britain constitute a 'social problem' for society.

However, it must be made clear that not everyone shares this view. For example, Brake and Hebdidge see different generations of youths as developing their own culture as a means of coping with their problems. Moreover, the styles young people develop merely reflect the particular cultural and economic circumstances of their class and generation.[63] Other observers argue that the emergence of such youth cultures is not just a strategy for coping but also carries a strong sense of resistance.[64]   It is perhaps that aspect which worries officialdom the most, as it threatens the status-quo. This was evident in Igor Ilynsky's comments in the previous chapter.

Youth as a continued social problem: juvenile crime in Russia and Britain

We have discovered earlier that official perceptions of youth are often negative, with teenagers seen to drink and smoke too much, take drugs and indulge in risky sex. However, as Griffin suggests, government policy-makers as well as researchers understanding of youth are influenced by their own ideologies and discourse.[65] The outcome of an older generation or, in Russia until Gorbachev, of a Gerontocracy, looking at teenage lifestyles, was that they frequently viewed them as a threat to society because of their rebellious, non-conformist attitudes and activities.   Nowhere is such a viewpoint more obvious than in the field of juvenile crime or delinquency.

As with the concepts of 'youth' and 'social problems' earlier, it is also essential to define 'juvenile delinquency'. Once again different cultural and societal factors affect this concept.   However, Cotsgrove provides a workable definition suitable for Britain and Russia. He argues that juvenile delinquency refers to 'that class of actions that when committed by a person under the age of 17 years, a particular society defines as attracting legal sanctions.[66]

Since the 1930s, the causes of delinquency have been variously located as differential association, rejection of middle-class norms and a lack of legitimate outlets for acts labelled as 'delinquent'. The trouble with all these viewpoints is that they accept stereotypical images of youth depicted above. More recently sociological theories, such as those of the social reaction or labelling school,[67] have stressed the fact that young people, especially working-class males, are labelled as deviant by those with the economic and political power to control the legal system. The suggestion made, therefore, is that social control agencies create deviance among the young because their actions - drinking, smoking, using drugs, having sex etc. - only become deviant when labelled as such.

Juvenile delinquency in Russia

In the pre-Gorbachev period, one of the main problems facing Western scholars studying crime was the shortage of statistics or else it was suggested that there was 'nothing in the nature of Soviet society which could give rise to crime'.[68] During Gorbachev's policy of 'glasnost', these earlier theories were largely abandoned and more sophisticated theories utilised, such as the view that crime was the product of a developmental process in which Russia was making a rapid transition from peasant to an industrial society; the result of anomie or finally the outcome of failures in the socialisation process.[69] As a result, it was now freely admitted that Russia had not created superior men or women but was merely suffering from the same difficulties as other major industrialised nations, such as Britain or the United States. Thus Shelley notes: 'One of the most alarming crime trends in the Soviet Union today is the increasing percentage of offences committed by juveniles'.[70] With regard to this statement, by 1988, 1.3m crimes were officially committed in the ex-USSR. Of this total, 710,000 were carried out by Soviet youth i.e. 15-30 year olds. Breaking this figure down still further, we find that 63,100 came from technical colleges, 47,400 from secondary schools and 14,200 from higher and specialised secondary educational establishments. Surprisingly, 127,000 of so-called juvenile delinquents were members of the Young Communist League (hereafter YCL).[71] The crimes committed by the young vary from theft of private property through to hooliganism. Taking the Soviet definition of youth, in 1988 young people were responsible for 56.6 per cent of embezzlements in the FSU; 33.4 per cent of thefts of state property; 41.2 per cent of premeditated murders; 41 per cent of grievous bodily harm cases; 86.7 per cent of rapes; 77.2 per cent of crimes against personal property; 33.6 per cent of speculators; 77 per cent of hooligans (which is much broader than disorderly conduct); 62.7 per cent of drug offences and 53.1 per cent of public transport and motoring offences. Young people here were persons under the age of 30 years.[72]

Trends in the post-Communist period have been far from encouraging. For example, in 1992, 2.76m crimes were committed and in the first six months of 1993 the total had already reached nearly 1.4m.[73] In 1993, criminals used weapons on 12,200 occasions and there were an estimated 150 mafia groups operating in Russia.[74] Coupled with this downturn in law and order since the collapse of Communism, there has been a corresponding increase in teenage crime. According to one *Komsomolskaia Pravda* reporter, 200,000 crimes were committed by young people in 1992. 100,000 of these were under the age of 14 at the time. All in all, according to Karmaza, between 1987 and 1993, the number of criminals aged 14-15 years rose by 50 per cent. As in the Communist period, most of these criminals (one in three) came from 'troubled families' in which many already had criminal records.[75]

In view of the above, crime and safety are high on the list of public concerns in the FSU. As Alexandr Golov of the Centre for Public Opinion Research (VTsIOM) in Moscow stated in July 1993: 'For the majority of our country's population, the most pressing problem right now is crime'.[76] Public opinion surveys carried out in June 1993 revealed that 36 per cent said hooliganism was very likely and 52 per cent thought it could happen. The corresponding figures for theft and robbery were 32 per cent and 51 per cent and those for organised crime 13 per cent and 31 per cent respectively. A further 25 per cent of those surveyed felt that underground wheeler-dealers or the mafia were in control of the *raion* or *gorod*.[77]

The situation depicted above has merely reinforced the mainstream view in both countries that youth constitutes a social problem no matter which aspect of their lifestyle we examine, be it drink, smoking, drugs, sex or crime.

Juvenile delinquency in Britain

In his book *Hooligan: A History of Respectable Fears* (1983), Geoffrey Pearson focuses on reactions to young criminals and he reaches the conclusion that the key to the problem lies in young people's loss of 'respect for authority'. He traces this problem not just back to the turbulent 1950s and 1960s, but to mid-nineteenth century Britain. But how accurate is such a view? According to Moore, the number of 14-20 year olds cautioned or found guilty of indictable offences in England and Wales increased from 63,000 in 1974 to 160,000 by 1984 among males and from 15,000 to 18,000 among females over the same period. He argues that the typical criminal in the UK is male, under 25 and usually of working-class origin.[78] Although the British government made law and order a priority, crime has continued to increase. Thus the crimes known to the Metropolitan police increased from 110,000 in 1952 to 625,000 in 1981 while the clear-up rate only rose from 40,000 to 100,000 over the same period.[79]   Part of the explanation for this lies in the fact that the underlying causes of crime - social deprivation; poor family socialisation; peer group influence at school, in the neighbourhood and at work - have been largely ignored. Instead, the Home Office in Britain has continued to occupy the high moral ground and used a *labelling process* with regard to young criminals.

The misrepresentation of youth?

The analysis presented above suggests that despite the different political situations in Russia and Britain, both societies have constantly identified youth as a social problem. However, the dominant theory has *mis-represented* youth in a number of respects. It assumes that all young people, irrespective of context, act in the same way and for the same reasons. Furthermore, the activities carried out by young people are *constructed* as a social problem in the sense that their behaviour is labelled as such. The consequence is that other causes of so-called deviant behaviour, such as the impact of poverty or socio-economic disadvantages on juvenile crime, are virtually ignored.

If we apply Western youth theories (as represented here by the case study of Britain) to Russia then, even if these theories are adapted to take the different cultural circumstances into account, the outcome would still be that we are exporting Western mainstream (sociological) thinking to the FSU. The consequence of this would be that dominant Western constructions of youth will now play an important part in the *social control* of young people's lives - their drinking, smoking, drug or sexual habits - in both countries. Discourses on youth in Russia and Britain will, therefore, continue to centre upon the notion of youth as a threat to society (respectable fears as suggested by Pearson) through the constant use of moral panics as indicated by Cohen.

While the emphasis among some sociologists was on resistance to conformity, as we saw in our discussion of youth culture, such a dichotomy is far too simplistic. Thus the focus in the youth crime context ignored fundamental questions pertaining to sexual orientation, gender, disability or race.[80] As young people are likely to continue dominating the policy and academic agenda for some time to come - either as a social problem or as the foundation of any society's future - these gaps and constant misrepresentations of the young need to be rectified. My aim here is not to present an alternative model, but to point to the flaws in existing governmental and academic analyses of youth in Russia and Britain. Once we have rejected the dominant stereotypical view that the behaviour of all young people is abnormal, excessive and deviant and hence a social problem for society, on the one hand, and youth begins to have an input, on the other, perhaps then, and only then will the West be able to help Russia.

Notes

1 J. Riordan, 'Soviet youth', in D. Lane (ed.), *Russia in flux: The Political and Social Consequences of Reform* (Edward Elgar, Aldershot, 1992), p. 149.

2 N. Timms, *A Sociological Approach to Social Problems* (RKP, London, 1967).

3 S. Cohen, *Folk Devils and Moral Panics* (Paladin, London, 1973).

4 This term is borrowed from M. Plant and M. Plant's book, *Risk Takers: Alcohol, Drugs, Sex and Youth* (Routledge, London, 1992). My indebtedness to them will soon become apparent to the reader.

5 B. Segal, *The Drunken Society: Alcohol Abuse and Alcoholism in the Soviet Union - A Comparative Study* (New York, Hippocrene Books, 1990); C. Williams, 'Old habits die hard: Alcoholism in Leningrad under N.E.P. and some lessons for the Gorbachov Administration', Irish Slavonic Studies, No. 12, 1991, pp. 69-96.

6 Segal, 1990 ibid., chapters 6-10.

7 Ye.V. Borisov and P.P. Vasilevskaia, *Alkogol' i deti* ('Meditsina', Moscow, 1981).

8 L. Roitman 'SSSR, alkogol i deti', *Nov. Russk. Slovo* 22 Sept. 1979.

9 V.V. Nagaev, 'Anketnoe issledovanie rasprostrannosti upotrebleniia alkogol'nykh napitkov', *Zdravookhranenie Rossiskoi Federatsii* (hereafter simply ZRF) 1971, No. 2 and V.V. Pashchenkov et al., *Nekotorye voprosy nasledstvennosti pri khronicheskom alkogolizme* (Moscow, 1972), p. 23.

10 Iu. Tedder and P. Sidorova, 'Vliyanie sem'i na otnoshchenie detei k potrebleniiu spiritakh napitkov', ZRF 1976, No.7.

11 I. Danshin and M. Kokotov, 'Izuchenie prichin prestupnosti', *Sotsialisticheskie zakonnost'* 1968, No.12.

12 Williams, 1991 op. cit.

13 Plant and Plant, 1992 op. cit., p. 19.

14 A. Marsh et al., *Adolescent Drinking* (HMSO, London, 1986), pp. 8-9.

15 Plant and Plant, ,1992, op. cit., p. 29.

16 Department of Transport, *Road Accidents in Britain: The Casualty Report* (Government Statistical Office, 1990), p. 25.

17 Home Office, *Offences of Drunkeness, England and Wales 1989* (Statistical Bulletin 40/90, London, 1990), p. 8.

18 Plant and Plant, 1992, op. cit., p. 61.

19 For more on this see C. Williams, 'The political economy of health care in the USSR', unpublished MSc (Econ) thesis, CREES, University College Swansea, 1986, Chapter 3.

20 I. Shalatonova et al., 'Shto pokazal opros potrebitelei tabachnykh izdelii', *Tabak* 1975, No. 3.

21 Williams, 1986, op. cit., p. 142.

22 K. Foster et al., *General Household Survey 1988* (HMSO, London, 1990).

23 Plant and Plant, 1992, op. cit., p. 63.

24 E. Goddard, *Why Children Start Smoking* (HMSO, London, 1990), p. ix.

25 Foster et al., 1990, op. cit., p. 115 and Plant and Plant, 1992, op. cit., p. 37.

26 P. Taylor, *The Smoke Ring: Tobacco, Money and International Business* (Sphere Books, London, 1985), p. xix.

27 M. Calnan, 'The politics of health: the case of smoking control', Journal of Social Policy, 1984, pp. 279-96.

28 Plant and Plant, 1992, op. cit., p. 40.

29 M. Schaeffer Conroy, 'Abuse of drugs other than alcohol and tobacco in the Soviet Union', Soviet Studies Vol 42 (3), July 1990, pp. 447-480.

30 J.M. Kramer, 'Drug abuse in the USSR', in: A. Jones et al. (eds.), *Soviet Social Problems* (Boulder, Westview Press, 1991), p. 97.

31 I. Kirillov, 'Potreblenie alkogolia i sotsial'nye posledviia p'ianstva i alkogolizma', *Vestnik statistiki* 1991, No. 6, p. 65.

32 *Izvestiia*, 27 June 1988.

33 *Komsomol'skaia Pravda*, 24 April 1993, p. 2.

34 *Izvestiia*, 16 February 1992, p. 6.

35 *Meditsinskaia Gazeta*, 25 June 1989, p. 2.

36 H. Swadi, 'Drug and substance use among 3,333 London adolescents', British Journal of Addiction, 1988, pp. 935-42.

37 Plant and Plant, 1992, op. cit., p. 68.

38 Ibid., pp. 69, 71.

39 Ibid., p. 72.

40 S. Moore and D. Rosenthal, *Sexuality in Adolescence* (Routledge, London, 1993), p. x.

41 C. Griffin, *Representations of Youth and Adolescence in Britain and America* (Polity Press, London, 1993).

42 I. Kon, 'Sexuality and culture', in I. Kon and J. Riordan (eds.), *Sex and Russian Society* (Pluto Press, London, 1993), pp. 15-44 and C. Williams, 'Sex education and the AIDS epidemic in the former Soviet Union', Sociology of Health and Illness 16 (1), January 1994, pp. 81-102.

43 I. Golod, 'Sociological problems of sexual morality', Soviet Sociology 13 (1), Summer 1969.

44 C. Williams, *AIDS in Post-Communist Russia and the Successor States* (Avebury, 1995).

45 Kon, 1993, op. cit., p. 35.

46 L. Attwood, 'Sex and the cinema' in Kon and Riordan 1993 op cit., pp. 65-66.

47 R.B. Dobson, 'Youth problems in the Soviet Union' in Jones et al. 1991 op. cit., p. 243.

48 N. Ford and K. Morgan, 'Heterosexual lifestyles of young people in an English city', Journal of Population and Social Studies 1989, pp. 167-85 and D. Foreman and C. Chilvers, 'Sexual behaviour of young and middle-aged men in England and Wales', British Medical Journal 1989, No. 239, pp. 1137-42.

49 Moore and Rosenthal, 1993, op. cit., p. 16.

50 B.J. Robertson and D.V. McQueen, 'Conceptions and misconceptions about transmission of HIV/AIDS among the Scottish general public, 1988-92', Health Bulletin 51 (5) September 1993, pp. 310-319.

51 cf. Plant and Plant, 1992, op. cit.

52 Moore and Rosenthal, 1993, op. cit., p. 16.

53 Plant and Plant, 1992, op. cit., p. 112.

54 M. Brake, *Comparative Youth Culture* (RKP, London, 1985).

55 S. Frith, *The Sociology of Youth* (Causeway Books, Ormskirk, 1984), p. 8.

56 J. Bushnell, *Moscow Graffiti: Language and Subculture* (Unwin Hyman, London, 1990); H. Pilkington, *Russian Youth and its Culture* (Routledge, London, 1994) and J. Riordan, *Soviet Youth Culture* (Macmillan, London, 1989).
57 L. Attwood, *The New Soviet Man and Woman: Sex-role Socialisation in the USSR* (Macmillan, London, 1990).
58 Riordan, 1989, op. cit.
59 M. Abrams, *The Teenage Consumer* (RKP, London, 1959).
60 J.B. Mays, *The Young Pretenders* (Michael Joseph, London, 1965).
61 Dobson, 1991, op. cit. and Riordan, 1989, op. cit.
62 S.N. Eisenstadt, *From Generation to Generation* (Free Press, Chicago, 1965).
63 M. Brake, *The Sociology of Youth Culture and Youth Subcultures* (RKP, London, 1980) and D. Hebdidge, *Subculture: The Meaning of Style* (Methuen, London, 1979).
64 See for example S. Hall and T. Jefferson, *Resistance Through Rituals* (Hutchinson, 1976).
65 Griffin, 1993, op. cit.
66 S. Cotsgrove, *The Science of Society* (Allen and Unwin, London, 1973), p. 141.
67 See for example, S. Box, *Deviance, Reality and Society* (Holt, Rinehart and Winston, 1981).
68 A.A. Gertsenzon, 'The community's role in the prevention of crime', Soviet Review 1960, No.1, pp. 14-27.
69 L.I. Shelley, 'Crime in the Soviet Union', in Jones et al., 1991, op. cit., p. 256.
70 L.I. Shelley, 'Crime and delinquency in the Soviet Union', in J.G. Pankhurst and M.P. Sacks (eds.), *Contemporary Soviet Society: Sociological Perspectives* (Praeger, New York, 1980), p. 220.
71 M. Ryan, *Contemporary Soviet Society: A Statistical Handbook* (Edward Elgar, Aldershot, 1990), pp. 166-67.
72 Ibid., p. 171.
73 *Izvestiia*, 12 February 1993, p. 5 and 21 July 1993, p. 2.
74 *Izvestiia*, 21 July 1993, p. 2.
75 *Komsomol'skaia Pravda*, 13 April 1993, p. 8.
76 *Izvestiia*, 23 July 1993, p. 4.
77 Ibid.

78 S. Moore, *Investigating Deviance* (Collins, London, 1991), pp. 129-30.
79 R. Kinsey et al., *Losing the Fight* (Blackwell, Oxford, 1986), p. 127.
80 See Griffin, 1993, op. cit., pp. 211-212.

3 Proto-democracy or proto-authoritarianism? Young people and the variants of post-totalitarian development

PETAR-EMIL MITEV

Introduction

The starting point of this chapter is that the prospects facing young people in Central and Eastern Europe (CEE) will depend on *security*, in international and domestic terms, and that security will be determined to a large extent by the interaction of two opposing trends: democracy and authoritarianism. The methodological point of departure of such a consideration is the hypothesis that integration on a world scale is not a uniform but rather a contradictory process. Integration does not imply a lack of disintegration processes, it rather implies the pre-eminence of the first over the second in the long run. Such an analysis necessitates special scrutiny of the differences between the countries of the region. The diversity of the erstwhile uniform societies of the Eastern Bloc, which are now resembling a 'dispersing galaxy', is an overwhelming, though still little studied fact.

Conceptual and theoretical considerations

In August 1989, prior to the start of the changes, the future President of Bulgaria Jelyu Jelev forecast a specific transition through the phase of 'fascism' in the dismantling of the communist totalitarian regime, with the reservation that 'it was highly probable that the transition through the specifically fascist stage may not be corroborated in all countries concerned'. Four years later, the prospect of evading the 'fascist' state appears to be so viable that the heuristic essence of the hypothesis is entirely forgotten and the issue is a turn from one of science into one of propaganda and ideology.

Today, naturally, there is a greater awareness of the availability of a broad range of options. The social experience of societies in transition is not synonymous. There are countries which have made major strides forward on the path of democratic development (Poland, the Czech Republic, Hungary, Bulgaria, the Baltic States). In retrospect, their societies are 'post-totalitarian', while in real prospect they are 'proto-democratic'. The proposition 'proto' designates not a lack of real democracy, but a factor of formation. Thus a fundamental fact in the system of political democracy is the Constitution, which exemplifies the social contract. Poland, however, does not have a new Constitution. Bulgaria has a new Constitution, but its legitimacy is vigorously contested. Both cases reflect the process of constructing a democratic system. A certain degree of uncertainty is a natural element of the legislative crisis related to transition.

In other countries (the ex-USSR countries in Asia or the Balkan states - Serbia, Croatia, Albania), the post-totalitarian set-up may soon be described as 'proto-authoritarian'. In this case, the term 'proto' is a time factor again. This does not mean that the regime of Milosevic in Serbia is an authoritarian one, rather it indicates that the authoritarianism itself is written into a dynamic regime holding a multiplicity of variables. Last but not least, there are the countries where democratic and authoritarian options stand in an intricate and mobile equilibrium (Russia and the Ukraine).

A key feature of Bulgaria has been the fusion of geopolitical reorientation with the type of decisions taken on key social, economic and political issues. This gives sufficient grounds, though relative, to resort to 'geographical' terms where alternative variants of development may be concerned.

Variants of development

The ongoing processes and variants of development, where they have become prevalent, may be variously described as: 'Americanisation', 'Europeanization', 'Slavization' and 'Orientalization' of the country. 'Europe' became the ideological symbol of return to a 'normal' (capitalist) development after a 45-year revolutionary 'departure'. And yet the ideological symbol, though sufficiently clear-cut by itself, appears to envelop diverse views and convictions and incorporate 'roads to Europe' that go through Washington and Istanbul. What we have in mind here is not simply priorities in foreign policy orientation, but types of societal development which incorporate geographical, domestic, socio-economic and socio-cultural aspects.

Americanisation

The Americanisation of Bulgaria is not reduced to 'particular' relations with the USA; it designates first and foremost the transfer of the American model of inter-relations between advanced and developing countries (with the reservation that Bulgaria is not an underdeveloped country, it has rather been a case of misdevelopment). Americanisation does not turn the country into a remote copy of the USA, it conversely approximates it to the structures and fate of the countries of Latin America. The 'Americanisation' is in fact a *'Balkano-americanisation'*, an analogy on the *'Latino-americanisation'*.

The following are the characteristic features of 'Balkano-americanisation':

- Excessive differentiation between rich and poor, which restricts or locks, or may ultimately annihilate democratic mechanisms and thus necessitates a 'strong hand';

- One-sided economic development on the basis of some agricultural or other type of primary resource; a 'Tomato' Republic (Chavdar Kuranov) or a 'Wild Plum' Republic (Yanko Yankov) to replace the Latin American 'Banana' Republic;

- Considerable political dependence of the country, despite an otherwise formal preservation of its sovereignty;

- A confrontational mode of political life; assertive rightist aggressiveness and ultra-left 'responses';

- Ideological intolerance; evolution of universal ideological tags to be used in the moral 'unmasking' and virtual removal of each and every political opponent;

- Diffident, inadequately stable and influential middle-class;

- Formation of a 'bureaucratic bourgeoisie' and influential compradore capitalism;

- Rightist policies in social welfare; limiting of trade union activity;

- Authoritarian or bordering on authoritarian rule (subordination of the judiciary and the media to executive power; synchronisation of the state and party structures; selection of cadres according to political 'loyalty' etc.);

- A 'strong hand';

- The USA assumes the role of 'Big Brother' and

- A brake on the processes of integration, which affiliate the country with the European Community, all disguised with 'European' phraseology.

Europeanization

The Europeanization of Bulgaria, even if it is to incorporate certain elements of the 'Balkano-American' variant, which were considered above, is basically distinct because possible involvement in European integration calls for compliance with the democratic standards of European structures and moral forms of political life.   Europeanization may have diverse emphasis ('Francophonian', 'Germanic' etc.) without ever questioning the priority of the European Community. (Naturally, the Europeanization will also be a *'Balkano-europeanization'*.) And yet there is a material distinction with Europeanization: europeanization of Spain also has a conditional feature and we call it 'Ibero-europeanization', but it is essentially distinct from 'Latino-americanisation'.

The characteristic features of europeanization are:

- Orientation of the major political forces on national consensus in the period of transition so as to minimise social unrest and avert hazardous situations; national reconciliation as the social and psychological prerequisite for a similar orientation;

- Regulation of the 'rich-poor' gap through a social policy framework (social funds, taxes etc.);

- The creation of a strong political centre, which successfully withstands the impact of centrifugal (extremist) political forces and guarantees the stability of democratic institutions;

- A stable middle class;

- A strong executive power within the framework of democratic institutions (*an authoritative President instead of an authoritarian General*) and

- A successful integration of the country within the European structures with a view to eventual admission to the European Community.

Slavization

The Slavization of the country represents a tendency towards the preservation and even enhancement of economic, political and cultural ties with the Slav countries (the number of which has sharply risen) and mostly with Russia as an assertive response, a retaliation against 'Westernization' and simultaneously a variant of economic and social formation involving:

- Priority of economic links with the countries of the Commonwealth of Independent States (CIS) and primarily with Russia and the Ukraine;

- Impact of the 'nomenklatura' version of post-communist transition, characteristic of certain Slav countries (Serbia, Russia), on the processes in Bulgaria;

- Slavophile form of the nationalist and leftist response to impoverishment and capitalist development;

- Positions of power and even dominance over the middle class of entrepreneurs and proprietors, linked with Russian capital;

- stable political position of the political formations with a Slav orientation and

- Powerful economic, political and social psychological presence of Russia.

Orientalization

The Orientalization of the country marks a trend towards the revival and growth of the relative impact of Oriental traits on the national character and public life of Bulgarians, encouraged or accompanied by:

- Priority of the 'Black Sea Economic Zone';

- Growing influence of the Middle East countries and especially of the 'Big Eastern Neighbour' on the economy, politics and culture of the country;

- Reduction of the 'change of system' to the replacement of faces and parties, to the 'dismantling of the totalitarian structures' in circumstances in which their socio-cultural, civic prerequisites have been fully preserved and even further consolidated;

- Demographic changes which enhance the presence of those groups burdened to the greatest extent with an Asiatic mentality (the 'Gipsyization');

- 'Turkification' of Bulgarians converted to Islam and

- A considerable 'Eastern' share in the composition and performance of the emerging middle-class.

Which path of development?

Each of the outlined trends, considered as a social process, is a reality in present-day Bulgarian society. However, their individual chances of gaining dominance varies. There are intricate relationships of inter-connection and mutual exclusion. In a *socio-cultural* sense, Americanisation and European-ization appear as various brands of 'Westernization', while the Slavization and Orientalization seem very close to Eastern models of development. But from the point of view of *geopolitical* re-orientation and *social and political* realities, an 'Orientalization' of the country could be carried out only under the auspices of and with the direct involvement of the USA; on the other hand, 'Americanisation' in the sense already indicated, not only does not exclude, it may even encourage the conservation of the Oriental encumbrance, as much as the Latin-American structures do not exclude but rather presuppose the exploitation of the psychology, mentality and traditions that have survived from pre-Columbus America. Any eventual support for 'Europeanization' on the part of the USA will be of particular significance and will help minimise security hazards in the region.

Impact on youth and youth policy

With the transition to democracy and a market economy, the range of prospects before young people is being abruptly transformed. The decisive stride forward (we may even describe that stride as revolution, though some tend to see it as counter-revolution) present opportunities for economic and social initiative. The transformation is paid for in different ways and also in different currencies when the old system of security of income has collapsed.

It has the following aspects:

-   Insecurity with regard to *life* and *property* against the backdrop of rising crime, reaching in certain circumstances the level of criminalization of social life.   According to a sociological poll carried out in Bulgaria in September 1993, crime accounts for some of the greatest worries and fears of parents in Bulgaria where their children are concerned (84 per cent);

-   Insecurity in terms of *health* and a healthy way of life.   According to the aforementioned poll, there are the risks, related to drug addiction (68 per cent) and alcohol abuse (63 per cent).   We could add here concern about substantial cuts in the public health system;

-   Insecurity in terms of *education*.   In the new economic climate (private education included) the fear of young people left without a proper education is increasingly real (one third of respondents support this view);

-   Difficulties regarding *employment*.   Young people (this applies to industrially advanced countries too) are increasing victims of unemployment and

-   Insecurity, resulting from political and/or ethnic *discrimination*.   Here we have both institutional and novel, non-institutional amateur forms of discrimination.

In a more general outline of *social and economic* development, the variants of transition from communism to democracy may be reduced to three models: nomenklatura capitalism; an open society or vulture capitalism. Let us consider each in turn.

Nomenklatura Capitalism

A portion of the former nomenklatura stratum is transformed into a new middle class and becomes a protagonist in the process of privatization and/or in the capacity of a 'bureaucratic bourgeoisie'; it then governs state property in a market economy. In terms of politics, there is a transition from a left-totalitarian to a left-authoritarian regime. Political pluralism is absent or is reduced to mere form. The dominant ideology is communism or communism transformed into socialism, nationalism.

An open society

An open society or 'Modern Capitalism' results with successful mass privatization, a balanced market economy and feasible cost of transition. In political terms, there is a stable political democracy, which is not jeopardised by the alternation of ruling parties or coalitions in the wake of democratic elections. The dominant ideology is liberalism, social liberalism.

Vulture capitalism

This occurs where furtive privatization assumes substantial proportions. Re-privatisation nurtures ambitions of revenge. The 'bureaucratic bour-geoisie' is again a protagonist, though of a different composition and orientation. In terms of politics, we have a right-authoritarian regime while the dominant ideology is anti-communism infinitum, nationalism.

We do not attempt here to provide a perspective of the individual models, even more so that the economic, political and moral evaluations will never coincide. Whatever the advantages of the nomenklatura model, its moral vulnerability is beyond question. To a certain extent, the left-authoritarian and right-authoritarian variants are mirror images. In both cases, the legislative crisis is purposely protracted, but is otherwise exploited by various social strata. The nomenklatura variant carries certain traits of 'vulture capitalism', while the latter enriches a bureaucracy of a 'new type'.

The flexibility of the situation in Bulgaria stems from the negation of the nomenklatura and the right-authoritarian variants, while the liberal one cannot be attained.

With different variants of transition, the problematic situation with which young people are faced becomes evident.

The nomenklatura variants, at least up to now, though being highly vulnerable owing to their origin, seem to offer the best chances for preserving employment. However, it may, at a certain point, go out of the control and 'bare' the teeth of 'vulture' capitalism. Two models have so far proved to be dirigible: the Chinese and the Serbian. In the first case, we have witnessed dramatic proof that the preservation of economic security occurs at the cost of social initiative. In the second, we have seen young people become carried away in a frenzy of nationalist sentiments, being ideologically and politically manipulated. Let us add that the Chinese experiment has not yet been carried through in order to be ultimately assessed.

The transition to an 'open society' seems optimal. However, the prerequisites for its materialisation are not always present; also we cannot say this is 'the best of all possible worlds'. And if the proto-authoritarian regimes have provoked the division of young people as a result of political affiliations and/or ethnic identification, the standard life-status stratification of young people is an inevitable characteristic of the transition to democracy. The good opportunities for all those who are capable of initiative and enterprise are there at the expense of economic inequality, often too flagrant in the aftermath of the communist system of all-levelling equality.

The post-totalitarian society needs, perhaps more than anything else, a *new work ethic* which endorses not only enterprise and entrepreneurship, but also work commitment; an ethic which does not reject but rather rationalises social inequality in labour relations. Egalitarian notions are deep-seated in the public consciousness and this is due not only to the last 45-years but to the traditions of left political culture, particularly in South Eastern Europe and Russia. The transition to a market economy and the emerging inequality may eventually come to intensify them. In this sense, what we have here is not only a momentum, a residual opposition to norms, included in the former basic consensus, but also a re-animation born of the prospect of development.

Society is in need of *new political morality* - the morality of freedom and responsibility, of tolerance and respect of law. After the totalitarian system, society was faced with a trying stock-taking, central to which is the issue of guilt and responsibility. This gave rise to aspirations for retribution, ambitions for revenge, desire to wreak vengeance. The problem, however, is not only subjective. The transition to democracy is in essence a *revolutionary process*. It cannot materialise through respect for valid laws, and in fact it gains momentum via the negation of the communist normative system. The distance spanning the vanishing authority of old laws and the as yet unestablished new laws has provided room for the manifestation of anomie and anarchy. There seems to be a vicious circle of sorts: the new political morality must evolve on the basis of adherence to law; the inculcation of new political morality passes through a phase of disrespect for the law. Naturally the contradiction appears, superficially, easy enough to handle if the definition of 'old' and 'new' laws is attached, but the problem is not so elementary. The forceful pressure with which the former laws and/or institutions are attacked is transferred in terms of perspective, thus creating a standard of wilful action. The cleaning of the 'Augean stables' of totalitarianism presupposes and requires radicalism, and radicalism does not sit easily with liberalism. The abrupt and powerful turn to the right has re-activated ultra-right movements, out-and-out fascist ones included.

The radical reappraisal refers not only to public norms and state institutions, political parties and their leaders. It runs deep into the *inner-world of the individual* as a compelling need for self-cleansing and stock-taking, as a problem of the relationship of the individual and his/her circle of friends, his/her family and conscience. If the wave of public negation surges to the 'summit' of the former hierarchical pyramid, to those who used to stand on official parade-day rostrums, it cannot fail to leave untouched the confidence, the conscience and the self-awareness of those who paraded at the foot of the rostrums. The culmination of the normative crisis is the problematization of personal identification. Political parties, public movements, trade unions and even sports organisations appear to split and multiply in a seemingly uncontainable process. In the same context, the rank-and-file individual is discovered, too, to be wavering between his own past and present, his 'authoritarian' and 'democratic' side. The search for truth about political ideas, parties and leaders logically ends with the discovery of the truth about oneself.

Conclusions

The values of present-day youth in the countries of the former Eastern Europe and Soviet Union are evolving in this complex situation. And each of the variants has not been spared its hardships and difficulties. The democratic variant is the optimal one not because it has been spared any hardships and controversies, but because it creates the optimal cir-cumstances for achieving the consensus, national consensus, needed to establish a new work ethic and new political morality in society.

The diversity of transition in its broadest international terms should be considered natural and even beneficial to security problems; in regional micro-terms, however, the prevalence of opposing variants in neighbouring countries may present a considerable hazard to international security. Suffice it to mention here the Balkans, following an eventual stable institution of left-authoritarian regimes in Serbia and Romania and right-authoritarian ones in Croatia and Albania.

The war in former Yugoslavia proved that the *domestic factors* of security are of decisive importance. The illusions of all who trusted in precedence as a result of foreign military intervention have been shattered. A military presence will lead to the consolidation, rather than the disintegration, of the authoritarian regimes in former Yugoslavia.

If we assume that the worst possible arrangement for the Balkans is the institution of *heterogeneous* authoritarian regimes in the neighbouring countries, then we should not be led to believe that *uniform* authoritarian regimes will be a better choice, free of controversies. In fact, they will all need an ideological motivation and disguise and we may never doubt that their ideology will be a nationalist one, irrespective of the political colouring of the national chauvinism.

There are no ready-made recipes for the transition from communism to democracy. The former socialist countries are moving along the path of 'trial and error'. Public insecurity, an unavoidable occurrence in the 'change of system' is enhanced manifold as a result of political strife merging with the process of privatisation; this will determine the economic elite of the country both in the short- and long-term. The struggle is being waged with a vengeance, with resort to heterogeneous ideological weaponry, and this introduces irrationalism into the situation.

To understand the problems and prospects facing young people today and changes in their scale of values during the transition, we need initially to disperse the ideological smoke-screen in order to be able to see things as they are and introduce greater sober-mindedness into social life.

PART II

RUSSIA AND THE CIS

4 State youth policy in Russia today

ANDREI SHARONOV

Introduction

I would like to describe state youth policy as an instrument of socialisation of the younger generation, in particular as an instrument of shaping the values and attitudes of young people. Because the issue chosen is very broad, I shall confine myself to just four aspects:

(i)   historical - what is the short history of state youth policy in Russia?

(ii)   psychological - how is this activity perceived by the Russian public and the authorities?

(iii) structural - how do the state youth policy institutions fit into the overall structure of state administration? and finally,

(iv)   technological - what instruments are there for achieving the aims of state youth policy?

Defining state youth policy

For a start, we already have an 'official' definition of state youth policy, as set down in the Main Lines of State policy, adopted by the Supreme Soviet of the Russian Federation on 3 June 1993. According to this document, state youth policy is defined as the state's actions in creating legal, economic and organisational conditions and guarantees in which a young man's or woman's personality may assert itself, and youth associations, movements and initiatives may develop. State youth policy reflects the state's strategy of socio-economic, political and cultural development as far as the younger generation is concerned.

Background

State youth policy in the Soviet Union dates from the late 1980s, when there was for the first time much talk about a Youth Law, in the wake of World Youth Year. Yet there is no doubt that youth policy in some form or another existed throughout the years of Soviet rule, ever since the Communist Youth League (*Komsomol*) was founded, since it became the country's only socio-political youth organisation and since Lenin spoke at its Third Congress. Its prime aim was to develop in young people a system of values and to integrate its institutions into a single youth organisation, whose membership at its peak was 48,000,000. Formally the Komsomol was not a Ministry of Youth, it functioned as something more than a ministry. One may differentiate four aspects of its work. First, it was the Communist Party's youth branch intended to inculcate official ideas into young minds and as the only channel through which young members could be recruited to the Communist Party; second, it was a wide-scale youth movement embracing most of the country's younger generation; third, it was a political youth organisation, especially during the final years of its existence when new political initiatives and movements emerged and finally, the Komsomol functioned as a state organ for youth, giving recommendations for certain kinds of activity, supporting literature and the arts, enterprise and tourism for young people, rallying together the young workforce, arranging holidays, law-enforcement, upholding legislation and other rights.

As a result, it was within the Central Committee of the All-Union

Communist Youth League that a draft law defining the status and ecological elements of state youth policy had taken shape in the mid-1960s, then in the 1970s, and finally in 1987-88. When the Soviet Union's Law on 'The General Principles of State Youth Policy in the USSR' was enacted in 1991, state youth policy was for the first time mentioned as a state activity, with non-state subjects involved in it. In May 1991, the Soviet Government's Committee for Youth was founded, but after the failed August 1991 coup, the ex-Soviet Republics shaped the course of this agency in their own individual ways. In Russia, a similar state structure, now known as the Russian Committee for Youth, was formed in August 1991. The Russian President's decree on 'Urgent Measures in State Youth Policy' was issued in September 1992. There followed the mainlines of State Youth Policy in which the Russian Government was given instructions to draw up amendments and additions to the current laws and then the draft programme 'Russian Youth' in June 1993. Also a vertical organisational structure became established during that period: of the 89 administrative constituents of the Russian Federation, 84 now have committees and divisions for youth, and at the level of towns and regions their number (including combined ones) is nearly 3,000. State youth policy is mainly paid from the budgets of all administrative levels.

This means we now have an organisation, legislative and financial foundation on which to implement state youth policy.

A gerontocratic legacy

Historically, gerontocratic traditions have always been strong in Russia. This is true of the Soviet period, when gerontocracy was based on a closed political elite and a strict hierarchy; this tradition goes all the way back to the time of the Tartar invasion. These traditions seem to be based upon the Oriental cult of age seniority and a rigid dependence of social status on age which is found in many aspects of Russian administration and general mentality.

Although much has changed, this still has a huge impact on state youth policies in Russia. Behind the slogan 'Young people are free to do anything', there is often nothing more than demagogy and political time-serving. Young people are generally taken seriously only when they have to be recruited in times of crisis, coups or elections. Many are still haunted by a post-totalitarian syndrome: youth policy is perceived as a left-over from the old regime, a kind of Komsomol nomenklatura invention intended to find a job for ex-Komsomol leaders. For the same reason, state youth policy is generally not taken as a kind of state activity: because the Komsomol and its followers have separated from the state, those who share this view believe that issues and problems of young people are issues and problems of civil society and its institutions only, such as public associations, parties, trade unions, the Church etc. Many people refer to the record of those countries in which a civil society has long been established, ignoring the fact that in the past 75 years, the state in Russia had stamped out any shoots of civil society.

Old versus new technocrats

Another new development showing how state youth policy is perceived is worth mentioning. This is the problem of 'old' and 'new' technocrats. To the first group belong President Yeltsin and Prime Minister Chernomyrdin (to a lesser degree though) and to the second shock therapy marketeers Boris Fedorov and Yegor Gaidar. My generation differentiation is based on how these politicians shape and treat principles of state administration. Leaving aside their specifics, the approaches of the 'old' and 'new' technocrats can be described as follows. 'Old' technocrats, as adherents to overall administration, have in mind social and, in particular, youth policies; Boris Yeltsin reveals his experience of Party work in which one had to pay much attention to young people, though in specific ways. 'New' technocrats do not like the ideas of total administration. They consciously limit the area of administration by regulating macro-economic links. Objectively, they accept the need for sufficient social policy, but subjectively, they look on it as a nuisance from the stand-point of revitalising the economy. This is especially true of state youth policy; they simply see it as being redundant.

Organisational issues

When we look at the structural aspect of state youth policy, we see that the establishment of statehood in Russia proceeds alongside an ongoing reorganisation of the state apparatus. In August 1991, three far-reaching attempts to reorganise the apparatus of ministries, government departments and the Council of Ministers were made, and five resolutions concerning the structure of youth work have been passed since then.

State building and youth policy

The reasons why such actions were taken seem to have been a desire to find an optimal structure of administration, a desire to settle political and personal issues through changes in the structure and a desire to gain real and faster results and reduce the size of the state apparatus.

The snag is that we have no concept of building a state apparatus in Russia, either on a Federal, regional or local level. The problem of Federal relations and the Federation's asymmetry makes this much more difficult.

Taking state youth policy as part of the state's general social policy, we think it reasonable to work out youth policy as a separate branch of the national economy. We have to establish young people's specific issues and interests in virtually all industries. Some issues will demand special organisation led by the Committee of Youth. Accordingly the structure of youth administration is a co-ordinated programme in which particular emphasis is given to horizontal connections and a non-hierarchical mode of vertical interaction. This type of organisation seems acceptable for various interdepartmental and interdisciplinary types of activity. For regional bodies, the Federal Committee is to co-ordinate, inform, recruit and employ and to adopt regulations, giving special emphasis to consensus-based relations.

Russia's social policy has too many passive, distributive measures addressed to the most deprived sections of the population and too few active measures addressed to creating conditions for self-help. This is especially important for able-bodied people, in particular young people, for whom good starting conditions are vital. We proceed from the principle of creating starting conditions for young people and we are seeking to implement that in programmes which support young people's innovative, imaginative and enterprising activities, thereby helping them to find employment.

Value system of young people

Let us now refer to the value system of young people today, the formation of values and their civic and patriotic training. There are actually no adequate institutions to deal with these vital issues, nor any institutionalised system under which such elements could be developed in the younger generation. This is another legacy of the transition from a totalitarian Party to a civil form of social organisation. In the Soviet Union, there was a rigid Party-controlled system of ideological education which indoctrinated Communist values into everybody from childhood to old age. The system has collapsed, and the idea of ideological education as a process of purposeful formation of a system of ideas and views in young people now seems desirable. The idea that moral and patriotic views and principles are in-born entities which cannot be infused from outside appears to have won the day.

It is tacitly assumed that family, school and Church must be the sources of the values of young people. But such social institutions are clearly in crisis. Neither family nor school seem able to oppose the flow of anti-human, demoralising attitudes pouring from the mass media. As long as there is no well-defined state policy in this field, this trend will continue. To rely on the Church in the present situation amounts to deceiving oneself, since most young people are only superficially or ritually interested in religion. So we find ourselves in a kind of vacuum where traditional institutions of socialisation, institutions of civil society are objectively unable to give young people moral and civic education and the state has not yet developed forms in which it can be involved in this process. The state's possible involvement, including that of the President (with his speeches to the nation and the younger generation), schools (with the emphasis on history and tradition), and rituals (the national flag, anthem and other symbols) will be the eventual solution. Incidentally, the Federal Programme 'Russian Youth', now under development, contains a section on patriotic education, but only two agencies - the Russian Committee for Youth and the Defence Ministry - are actively involved in it.

Implementing state youth policy

What instruments can we avail ourselves of in implementing state youth policy?

On a legislative level, the Main Line of State Youth Policy is one of the instruments. The Russian President's Decree No. 1075 has fulfilled its function, having instituted the Russian Committee of Youth, having recognised the National Council of Youth Associations of Russia, having created a precedent of state financial support for youth and children's organisations and having stimulated similar processes at a local level.

Strictly speaking, the Main Lines of State Youth Policy are not a legal act; they are 'conceptual principles on the basis of which state youth policy is to be formed and implemented in Russia. The aims and principles of state youth policy are common to all levels of state power and administration. Bodies of state power and administration are responsible for implementing measures in state youth policy, relying on regulations and programmes they adopt within their competence'.

This wording has been chosen on the basis of the Federation Agreement, under which social policies are matters of joint and local competence and only principles of policy can be adopted on a Federal level.

The Main Lines of State Youth Policy are continuing in the form of amendments and additions, now in preparation, to the current laws. First of all, there are criminal procedure laws, laws on marriage and the family, social associations law, taxation law and so forth.

Preparations for the 'Russian Youth' Federal Programme are near completion. It consists of four programmes: 'Establishing an information system for young people', 'Tackling social and economic youth problems', 'Forming conditions for the spiritual and physical development of youth' and 'Supporting the activity of children's and youth organisations'. The 'Russian Youth' programme is planned for 1994-97 and will embrace key issues associated with programmes now in force or under development.

Youth policy programmes have been adopted in most of Russia and some laws on youth policy exist in some of the Russian Federation's republics (for example, Bashkortstan and Chuvashia). Furthermore, the Board of the Russian Committee for Youth has approved the 'Regulations on partial funding of children's and youth organisations' through which some 30 programmes on a Federal level were supported in 1993.

5 Russian youth in a transient society

BORIS RUCHKIN

Introduction

Russian reality affirms the truth of Stendhal's statement made many years ago to the effect that there comes a time when policy is identified with destiny. Russian society and youth are doomed to 'stew in the pot' of political passions for a long time to come since successful political change depends in many ways on the solution of economic problems. The tragic events in Moscow of 3-4 October 1993 (the 'storming of the White House') did not consolidate society on the way to civil peace or elections for a new parliament. All the problems and grounds for serious political crises will continue to remain in Russia for an indefinite span of time. Youth, as an important social force, should not be ignored when questions of the future and its own problems are being tackled.

Background

According to the logic of events, youth should *not* be ignored. However, the latest youth studies once again show that throughout the eight years of perestroika and the post-perestroika period, the creation of acceptable social conditions for the younger and subsequent generations is not considered to be important at all. From a historical stand-point, such a policy can be said to be irresponsible, even if we take into consideration the fact that this is not being done deliberately, that it is not an objective and that nobody wishes to implement an *anti-youth policy*. However, the results of numerous studies and surveys lead us to the conclusion that 'youth is invariably allotted the last, lowest step in the hierarchical ladder of the political system'. Statistics and sociology speak of the dismissal of youth from power.

Youth, socialism and the continuity of generations

Together with society in general, youth is going through a period of change in its ideological, economic and moral values and this is determining its political direction. This means that the natural, normal course of inter-generation continuity has been broken. One of the most striking changes is that of attitudes to the concept of 'socialism'. In the course of perestroika, society began to divide into the supporters of socialism and its opponents. Society in growing measure took the road of ideological (and that means political) struggle. In the long-term over the last few years, this struggle turned into the 'putsch' or 'coup'. The Moscow events vividly showed *two peoples*: those who stood by the Russian 'White House' and those who, on the call of Gaidar, came to defend the Moscow Soviet. Within the context of our theme, the problem of 'socialism' is closely connected with the problem of conflict, contradictions of generations, when questions of history are in keeping with present problems and follow the simplified pattern of 'Are you for or against me?'

We should first of all note that a re-estimation of values on the part of youth occurred within a relatively short historical period. Already in 1983 (according to the data of many studies), 84 per cent of young people of the USSR were convinced that socialism actually brought the most important social and political rights.[1] By 1993, according to our research, socialism had lost its attraction for the overwhelming majority of young people. In the consciousness of youth, old values did not retreat in a linear way, yet they retreated firmly enough. Thus in 1990, 17 per cent of interviewed students believed in the inevitable victory of communism, while in 1992 the figure had dropped to 5 per cent (according to the survey 'Children of Russia').

The 19th century philosopher Alexander Herzen, who admitted that at some future date socialism would develop 'to the level of extreme consequences and absurdities', predicted the crisis of socialism. He stated, 'Then the cry of negation will again burst from the titanic bosom of the revolutionary minority, and once more there will be a mortal struggle in which socialism will replace contemporary conservatism which will in its turn be conquered by the coming revolution.' This did not all coincide with our notions since, following Marx, we perceived socialism to be a many-sided and absolute solution of social problems.   It continues to be an invariable value in the eyes of a substantial proportion of the older generation of the country, and of the parties and movements which still follow communist doctrine.

However, through the efforts of advocates of capitalist development, entire historical periods, together with the historical experience of a number of generations, are being cast out of history. Super-negation of all things and persons cannot but tell on the consciousness of the growing generation, in whose eyes the older generation is a dogmatic, conservative group guilty of all the misfortunes which have befallen Russia. Without dwelling on the consequences of such a policy, we should stress the fact that in conditions of the transient moment, the *breaking* of the chain of generations may become a reality. What is more, it can lead to a sharp conflict between them.

The reading of history in a way that would please the powers-that-be is a fatal mistake, the more so since the question of the future of socialism remains unresolved.   In his writings the Russian religious philosopher Berdyaev stated: 'The problem of socialism, which has world significance, is extremely complex and has many aspects. The metaphysical and spiritual aspect of socialism and its social and economic aspects should be assessed differently.' Only 'a certain inner truth' of socialism could make some hearts beat more quickly and fervently and fire the masses with enthusiasm.[2]

Socialism as a reality remains in the consciousness not only of the older generation, but, to a certain extent, of youth too. According to our survey conducted in late 1992, 9 per cent of young people (22,600 persons were interviewed) wanted to live in a socialist society, 34 per cent in a capitalist society and 47 per cent in some other society. Moscow played host on 29-30 October 1993 to the international conference 'Scholars for Democracy and Socialism'. Participants from the USA, Great Britain, Italy, Denmark and Russia analysed the reasons for the global crisis of socialism. At the same time, they presented arguments for the inevitability of its revival on the grounds of rejection of totalitarianism and its replacement by the principles of free association and self-government.[3]

Summing up these statements, we should underline that we must not in our historical analysis expose as manifestations of mere foolishness the victims, the ups and downs, the mistakes and miscalculations of those who built socialism in the 20th century. In regard to the relations between generations, *continuity* should serve as the basis for their development while the mistakes of the past should be taken as a lesson for future generations. In any solution to the problem, we should rely on the international experience of countries which have already passed from dictatorship to democracy and a market economy - for example, Spain after Franco's death.

Reforms, revolution and youth

'We seem to live in order to provide humanity with a great lesson' (Chaadaev).

What is actually happening in Russia today - reform or revolution? Comprehension of the process of political change in society predetermines, among other things, the behaviour of youth and its attitudes to these changes.

Revolution is generally understood to be the overthrowing of a state by the people; they view themselves as the rulers of a new historical destiny. If we follow such an interpretation, what we actually see in Russia today is not a revolution. Actually the restructuring of the system, which began in 1985, was intended to revitalise socialism, to give it a 'human face'. However, this was followed by the withdrawal of Russia from the USSR, embarking on a course for building capitalism, destroying parliament and with it, according to the President, 'the inglorious end of the Soviets'. We agree with A.S. Askoldov, who said that every major historical crisis, which brings a clash of internal state relations, is a revolution.[4]

An analysis of political change in these years shows that what we are witnessing today is not a process of improvement in the former system, but its dismantling. The 1993 'coup' was accomplished at the top. Further, it turned into a *long spontaneous revolution*. In the course of the revolution, political institutions and laws existed as long as they enjoyed the support of a *substantial proportion of the population or they relied on coercion.*

Precisely in this context, it is important to know if youth carries within it new social relations in the building of a new society. The question is particularly pertinent to the period after the 'October' 1993 events in Moscow.

The strength of power lies in trust

The question posed after the October events 'Can the politicians who rule today cope with the problems facing society?' received the following answers: 'Yes' - 20.5 per cent (persons aged 18-24 years); 21 per cent (those 30-34); 30 per cent - farmers; 28 per cent - businessmen; and 20 per cent - students. The corresponding figures for those saying 'No' were 56 per cent; 61 per cent; 58.6 per cent; 59.4 per cent and 60 per cent respectively. The most trusted institutions of power were, as before, the Armed Forces, and particularly the Church.

The lack of trust in present-day politicians is due to many reasons. Not least is the fact that all three branches of power did not seriously engage in implementing a State youth policy; the solution to youth problems lies beyond the terms of reference of the Russian Youth Committee. Youth found itself a victim of political separatist and nationalist ambitions; it is the first to make sacrifices in endless inter-ethnic conflicts. In Nagorno-Karabakh alone, 21,000 young people have been killed. We should also add that throughout these eight years, young people heard many promises from the authorities and met as many disappointments. As many as 48 per cent of those interviewed perceived the 1993 events in Moscow as negative, while 33 per cent considered the political situation to be much worse than it was on the eve of these events. A large proportion of the younger generation has come to the conclusion that neither present-day politicians, nor their decrees, can swiftly solve the country's problems. The transformation of society is a long and extremely dangerous process, which has only just begun.

Young people are coming to understand that a change of political generations is inevitable.

In the course of our survey, over 70 per cent of all voters, including 80 per cent of the young, stated that they were in favour of the rejuvenation of representative and executive bodies. One third of the voters showed a preference for politicians of the younger generation (under 35) and 64 per cent for politicians of the middle generation.

An analysis of the list of candidates for the new parliament, presented by 13 Associations and Blocs, shows that political leaders are also aware of the need for rejuvenation. Of the 1,755 initially nominated candidates, 344 were persons under 35 years (19.6 per cent), excluding candidates nominated by the bloc 'The Future of Russia - New Names'; the figure fell to 66 persons or nearly 17 per cent. Yet only a few of them were elected and mainly persons over 40 came to power.

The position of youth in the Federal power structures continues to be inadequate compared with its social significance in society in such a critical period.

Youth and social peace

The Referendum conducted on 25 April 1993 clearly showed the split in society. Some 38 per cent of citizens (40.4 million) showed their political commitment to the President, while 25 per cent (27 million) opposed. Naturally, these political feelings were based on an economic response to the 'shock therapy': 30.6 million do not actively accept this economic policy against 36.5 million who support it. Of the number of young people interviewed, 32 per cent assessed the results of the Referendum negatively, as factors which can only lead society to further division. The social balance in society determines the character of political actions realised after April - the search for reserves, allies and scandals ... All these activities brought about the events of 3-4 October. Those who used tanks first conquered power.

However, the question of social support in implementing reforms and of social stability has not yet been decided.

Where do the powers-that-be look for support? The ideologist Burbulis states: 'Today the structures of executive power rely on and are oriented to the rapidly growing class which is at the same time quickly becoming wealthy'.[5] This means that from the very beginning the interests of a small section of the population are put above all other interests. If such a policy is pursued it will be difficult to expect social reconciliation. Aristotle once said that only those states in which intermediate people are great in number have a good system, for when some people possess too much and others have nothing, we have either extreme democracy, oligarchy in its pure form or tyranny, which comes under the influence of opposite extremes.[6]

The success of a policy oriented on the middle-class majority, in post-war conditions, was demonstrated by Chancellor Erhard in West Germany. His reforms were supported by rank-and-file Germans; in other words, they met with wide social support. As regards Russian reality, research shows that only a minority of young people make up the small proportion of businessmen (2.5 per cent of those interviewed) and those intending to go into business (about 30 per cent) who are taking part in the economic reforms. The findings of our study show that the protracted 'shock therapy' methods move young people to take a conservative stance. From 40 per cent to 70 per cent (depending on the category of youth) hold a negative attitude to the reforms. We have a paradoxical historical situation where the psychological characteristics of young people which are so necessary for social development are being ignored by society; yet there exists a real danger that youth will become an obstacle to the renewal of Russia.

Youth, as before, is not the direct social basis of the economic transformation that is being brought about today.

Conclusions

The substantial changes in policy have broadened the area of political activity intended to resolve youth problems. Formally this is so. At the same time, however, political changes and reforms have strongly aggravated the socio-economic position of youth and this has been only slightly taken into account in the policy being carried out by the authorities. Nevertheless, it is precisely the factor of the younger generation which can give social progress the needed impetus, which can make society more stable.

A social explosion of youth can be averted by pursuing a responsible youth policy. The chief idea of the Russian reforms and development should be not merely a 'market economy', taken in isolation from the individual, but the individual him/herself, an individual who understands the meaning of the reforms, and participates in them. This must involve first and foremost the young individual as the bearer of the future, the source of innovation and change.

It is imperative today to draw young people into politics. The last eight years have not created a new generation of politicians. The main task today is to create a mechanism of representation of youth in all branches of power, to develop a model of youth participation in political life under democratic conditions. In this respect, the experience of the pre-election struggle, in which the bloc 'The Future of Russia - New Names' was engaged, deserves special attention.

As regards State Youth Policy it can be briefly summed up as follows. Recently some major positive advances have been made, as shown in the previous chapter. However, they came *late* and today it is not clear how effective the political influence of the Russian Youth Committee will be in implementing the measures outlined in the previous chapter.

In the near future, the political space for youth will broaden. This is because political blocs and parties in their fight for mandates have to seek support from the younger generation. However, the key point here is who in all this diversity will take upon himself the task of tackling the real problems of the young. What can young people regard as worthwhile in the youth policies presented by these blocs in their political manifestos?

Notes

1   *Mir Filosofii* (World of Philosophy), Part II (Moscow, 1991), pp. 482-83.
2   Cited by P.I. Novogorodtsev, *Ob obshchestvennom ideale* (On the social ideal) (Moscow, 1991), p. 207.
3   *Pravda* 18 November 1993.
4   See the collection *Iz Glubiny* (From the Depth) (Moscow, 1991), p. 9.
5   *Izvestiia* 15 October 1993.
6   Cited in *Mir Filosofii* 1991 op cit., p. 415.

6   The rise and fall of a youth elite in Russia

JAMES RIORDAN

Rise and fall of Soviet youth organisations

In the mid-1980s, the Soviet children's and youth movement embraced virtually all schoolchildren; it had no rivals, and the values it sought to instil fully coincided with those of all other officially-approved socialising agencies. Its goals were explicitly political and the entire movement was tightly controlled by the Communist Party.

The three-link chain of the movement encompassed young people from the age of seven to 28 years, as follows:

1.   The Octobrists (*Oktyabryata*) - 7-9 years;
2.   The Pioneers (*Pionery*) - 10-14 years; and
3.   The Young Communist League (*Komsomol*) - 14-28 years.

Almost all children in the relevant age groups were members of the Octobrists and/or Pioneers. Komsomol membership, however, was roughly 60 per cent of the 14 to 28 year olds, with formal affiliation diminishing with age.[1]

The Pioneers led the Octobrists, the Komsomol led the Pioneers, and children moved from one step of the ladder to the next as they grew up. It is no exaggeration to say that the children's and youth organisations dominated the lives of their members and were a major influence on all young Soviet people. Well over 200 million young people passed through their ranks. Internationally, their influence rivalled that of the Scouts, embracing all continents and major powers, their prototypes ranging from China to Cuba, Zimbabwe to Chile, Britain to the USA. The Pioneers and the Komsomol, therefore, cast a giant shadow over millions of young people the world over.

Within the USSR, as recently as 1987, the Pioneers aspired to involve *all* nine to 14 year olds, and the Komsomol aimed 'to cover the entire younger generation' inasmuch as 'constant growth in the Komsomol ranks is a sign of successful activity and authority among young people'.[2]

Yet, within the space of a few years, not only was the monopoly of the Party-controlled youth organisation broken; it began to disintegrate rapidly. In September 1990, the Pioneers formally broke with the Komsomol and Party, becoming the Federation of Children's Organisations which firmly rejected politics and ideology, swapped its red for blue neckerchiefs, and its old Boy Scout motto 'Be Prepared' for the new 'For Country, Goodness and Justice'. It also had to contend with a number of rivals, including the re-formed Russian Scout movement.

As for the Komsomol, its rapid disintegration commenced in 1990, with the mass exodus of certain ethnic groups (e.g. in Georgia, Armenia, Moldova and Azerbaidzhan) and the bulk of Lithuanian, Estonian and Latvian members (the Estonian Komsomol dissolved itself; the Latvian and Lithuanian was confined to non-Balts). Even in Russia, the Komsomol adopted a new red-white-and-blue flag and exchanged its Lenin Badge for one bearing a gold birch leaf. If that were not enough, a break-away group set up the Russian Democratic Socialist Youth Association that rejected Marxism. Finally, following the failed coup of 19-22 August 1991, the Komsomol, having dwindled from 42m to 19m members since 1985, decided to disband at an extraordinary congress on 27-28 September 1991.[3]

It should be noted in parenthesis that a relatively small group (about 250) young communists, backed by former conservative Politburo member Yegor Ligachov, resolved to resurrect the All-Union Lenin Communist League at a two-day congress held outside Moscow on 19 April 1992. The new Komsomol 'would be truer to the original revolutionary Komsomol than its pre-coup counterpart'.[4]

The demise of the old Komsomol naturally came in the wake of the dismantling of all communist structures in the old edifice of the USSR. The interesting fact, however, from several surveys held in the late 1980s was not that the Komsomol was unpopular, but that it was *the most unpopular institution in Soviet society* - more so than the Party, KGB or Trade Ministry.[5] The lack of trust came partly from the fact that it was perceived as ignoring the interests of young people. Komsomol leaders were seen as being more concerned with feathering their own nests than attending to youth concerns.

Partly, too, lack of popularity was due to the process of perestroika undermining the prestige of all official institutions, the Komsomol included. Those who had set themselves up as moralisers had to expect more than mild strictures when their own standards fell or they were caught transgressing. As the revelations mounted of the Komsomol's implication in the crimes of the past (personality cult, purges, extermination of all opposition, distortion of history, stagnation, links with the security forces), so the revulsion grew. It will not have escaped attention that two previous Komsomol leaders (Semichastny and Shelepin) went on to become security chiefs or, as the 21st Komsomol Congress (April 1990) materials revealed, that 42,000 Komsomol members were still employed by the KGB.[6]

As young people's involvement in all manner of informal groups burgeoned, so activity in 'formal' groups like the Komsomol plummeted in the late 1980s. Some young people, freed from the social pressures of the Komsomol, evidently sought an outlet for their energies in juvenile delinquency and drug taking. Others sought enterprise and opportunity in co-operative business (see chapters 1-2). There were also those politically active young people who found no means of expression within an unreceptive and initiative-less Komsomol, and were seeking a place in one of the many political groups that sprang up in the early 1990s.

Before examining the Komsomol elite, it is worth taking a backward glance at how exactly the Komsomol came to develop, for in many ways it mirrors the growing decrepitude and corruption that beset other, non-youth, political and social organisations.

At the official birth of the Komsomol, 29 October - 4 November 1918, as many as 194 delegates representing 120 youth groups met in Moscow at the First Congress. It is noteworthy that while the Congress 'expressed solidarity with the Russian Communist Party', it also declared the Komsomol to be 'an independent organisation'.[7] Indeed, its first rules reiterated that it was a 'fully independent organisation' whose activities were based on 'the principle of complete freedom of action'.[8] Such autonomy was not to last long under Civil War conditions. In the following year, the word 'independent' was erased and, at the Third Congress, held in October 1920, at which Lenin spoke, the 'freedom of action' principle vanished.

Similarly, relative freedom of election to top posts gave way to Party control or nomination. Up to 1920, members elected the Central Committee by voting for nominees individually; and since there were more nominees than posts, an element of choice obtained. In 1920, the choice was removed: delegates to the Third Congress were presented with a single list of nominees drawn up in advance by the Party, with only one nominee for each vacancy. Delegates had to vote on the list *as a whole*.

From then up to 1990, no real elections took place, not only to the Central Committee, but to the secretaryships of local committees as well. In fact, from its Central Committee down to its smallest branch, the Komsomol functioned under direct Party tutelage; and since the leading Komsomol officials were invariably themselves Party members, they were always subject to Party discipline and removable on Party command. One Komsomol leader, Alexander Kosarev, was even a Party Politburo member. All first secretaries (the de facto leaders) of the Komsomol were automatically co-opted onto the Party Central Committee, and all ideology secretaries to candidate membership of the Party Central Committee.

If that were not enough to ensure Party control, the Party over the years arbitrarily removed Komsomol officials and leaders whenever it wished; that included the mass arrest and execution of virtually the entire Komsomol leadership during the Stalin purge years (of the first seven Komsomol leaders between 1918 and 1938, six were shot and one, Milchakov, spent 14 years in a Magadan labour camp) (see Table 6.1 below).

Although the principle of Komsomol organisation, 'democratic centralism', was from the outset far more centralist than democratic, and remained so right up to 1991, early Komsomol meetings gave vent to dissension and the initial congresses produced many divided votes. Even during the early 1920s, the Komsomol in its activities was still relatively independent and members could register dissenting votes; even sharp criticism of arbitrary rule within the organisation could still be mentioned in the published record. But even this limited freedom to demur vanished by the mid-1920s. The Komsomol could not dare question in the slightest degree the supreme authority of the Party. Voting on all issues became mechanical and any dissenters (or supposed dissenters) were removed. The Komsomol was the first organisation to be purged (for its alleged 'Trotskyist leanings'). Not even abstentions from voting were recorded at congresses after 1926 and this remained so until the 20th Congress in 1987.

Table 6.1
First secretaries of the Russia Komsomol, 1918-91

Yevgeny Tsetlin (1918)	shot
Oscar Ryvkin (1918-19)	shot
Lazar Shatskin (1919-22)	shot
Pyotr Smorodin (1922-24)	shot
Nikolai Chaplin (1924-28)	shot
Alexander Milchakov (1928-29)	14 years in camp
Alexander Kosarev (1929-38)	shot
Nikolai Mikhailov (1938-52)	
Alexander Shelepin (1952-58)	
Vladimir Semichastny (1958-59)	
Sergei Pavlov (1959-68)	
Yevgeny Tyazhelnikov (1968-77)	
Boris Pastukhov (1977-82)	
Victor Mishin (1982-86)	
Victor Mironenko (1986-90)	
Vladimir Zuikin (1990-91)	

Sources: *Bolshaya Sovetskaya Entsiklopediya*; R. Medvedev, Let History Judge (London, Macmillan, 1972), pp. 208-9; Alexander Kosarev, *Sbornik vospominanii* (Moscow, 1963); *Vozhaki Komsomola. Sbornik* (Moscow, 1978); *Sobesednik* July 1986, no. 30, p. 20; *Komsomolskaya Pravda* 11 June 1988, pp. 2-3; A.A. Alexeyev et al. (eds), *Stroka v biografii Sekretari Tsentralnovo Komiteta Komsomola 1918-1990gg* (Moscow, 1990).

Initially the Komsomol was very small, the largest membership during the founding period being some 400,000 - that is, under 2 per cent of those within the eligible age group and two-thirds the size of the Party.[9] Like the Party it aimed to recruit only 'outstanding representatives' and had no pretensions at embracing all young people, even if that were possible. Although favoured by the ruling Party, it had to vie for members and attention with surviving pre-revolutionary youth organisations like the Boy Scouts, the YMCA, the Jewish Maccabee and various religious youth groups. It was not until 1922 that such rivals were proscribed, although the 7th Komsomol Congress in 1926 still mentioned the existence of 'leagues of Christian youth' and other non-communist youth associations.[10] From 1926, however, the Komsomol had the field to itself.

The tasks of the Komsomol were set by the Party as early as March 1919. It was to be a 'source of trained reserves for the Party' and to help the Party implement its policies. It was 'to organise and train young people in a communist manner, to build a communist society and to defend the Soviet Republic'.[11] In the years to follow, the Komsomol retained many of the characteristics it had acquired under Civil War conditions - its organisational structure based on democratic centralism, its role of replenishing the Party with young recruits, of political socialisation of young people and of helping the Party to carry out its policies, as well as its political control by the Party. On the other hand, from being a tiny 'vanguard' of youth, it became a mass organisation; it shifted its organisational base from home to school and workplace. And from the mid-1920s until the late 1980s it had no formal rivals, nor were dissent, independent initiative or free elections permitted.

Despite glasnost it was not until 1988 that the Komsomol theoretical journal *Molodoi kommunist* (subsequently to change its name to *Perspektivy*) admitted the murder by the regime of its early leaders. What the journal failed to state was the connivance of the Komsomol and Party hierarchy in their murder, or their own far-from-pure records of repression. The victims often began as zealous participants in the Terror before a sense of their own danger finally prompted them to resist.

Relationship with the party

The relationship between the Komsomol and the Communist Party is yet another legacy of the past. Lenin had made no bones about the fact that in his view, 'We must unreservedly be in favour of complete independence of the youth leagues' (note the plural); after all, 'without complete independence young people will not be able either to become decent socialists or to prepare themselves to take socialism forward'.[12]

How did recent Komsomol and Party leaders view this Party-Komsomol relationship? At the 20th Komsomol Congress in 1989, Gorbachov stated that the Party 'understands leadership over the Komsomol in the sense of the Komsomol giving us constant comradely support; we see that as the Komsomol's main duty'.[13] At the 21st Congress in 1990 he was equally unambiguous, though inclining towards close relations: 'We want to see the political youth organisation in step with the Party, working together with it'. When asked about the Komsomol being the Party's 'reserve', however, he was forthright: 'The Party cannot function properly if the communist youth organisation is not in step with it. Call it a reserve or helper, if you like, but the Party cannot operate properly without it. It must replenish its ranks from among Young Communists'.[14]

Nowhere did he mention the Komsomol ceding its monopoly position in respect of young people (*the* issue concerning youth). His words would hardly convince young people that the Komsomol was no longer an arm (or, as they often saw it, 'a mailed fist') of the Party.

How did Komsomol leaders themselves see the Party-Komsomol relationship in the new circumstances? At its 8th plenum in August 1989, the Komsomol Central Committee stated categorically that 'the Komsomol recognises the political leadership of the Party, decisively and firmly supports the CPSU as the political vanguard of society' - voting being 182 for, one abstention, none against.[15] It further based the Rules 'on Marxist-Leninist method and analysis of social development; it shall conduct its activity on the basis of the same ideological platform as the CPSU' - voting being 175 for, three abstentions, none against.[16] All that despite the clear message from public opinion surveys among young people that: 'An absolute majority of Komsomol members (58 per cent) are in favour of the Komsomol becoming a fully independent organisation and an equal partner in relations between Party and state'.[17]

One may justifiably ask how the Komsomol could be independent of the Party when 80 per cent of Komsomol officials were Party members. And every Party member was obliged to carry out all Party decisions. In fact, at the 21st Congress of the Komsomol, as many as 78.3 per cent of the delegates were in the Party or were Candidate members;[18] it was their duty to carry out Party policy, and in no way could they be independent of it.

However, cracks began to appear in the Party-Komsomol edifice. In mid-1990, Stanislav Smirnov, a recent candidate for Komsomol leadership and then Russian Supreme Soviet Chairman on Youth Affairs, was dismissed from the Party for advocating the de politicisation of Russian schools. The Komsomol responded by creating a new post for Smirnov, making him effectively the Komsomol's second-in-command.

The Komsomol elite: a system within a system

The problem of any well-established organisational leadership without competition is that, having tasted the fruits of power and privilege, it is reluctant to give them up and always finds a thousand and one 'ethical', 'economic' and 'political' arguments for retaining the status quo, stressing the notorious 'need for continuity' (*preemstvennost*).

In the last few years the accusation gathered momentum that the Komsomol was 'a state within a state', a system within a system. Maria Pastukhova, herself a member of the Komsomol Central Committee Bureau, wrote that: 'The Komsomol Central Committee is a state within a state. Many people see the Komsomol as a nest of gentry of political functionaries rather than as *their* organisation'.[19]

A group of leading Komsomol members called the Komsomol 'An entire state within a state, with a smooth-running machine of rank and privilege, a strict, ramified hierarchy of jobs, unwritten rules and traditions'.[20]

Most damning of all was a report by Victor Graivoronsky, first secretary of Moscow's Gagarin District Komsomol Committee, in the Moscow Komsomol daily *Moskovsky komsomolets*. He termed the Komsomol apparat the 'System' (*Sistema*) whose core constituted 'more than a hundred thousand strong apparatus (one functionary to over 250 ordinary Komsomol members) on whose maintenance is spent the astronomical sum of 400 million roubles.[21] Graivoronsky detailed the extensive material privileges of the 'System': over 1,300 people in the apparat of the Komsomol Central Committee received an average salary of between 350 and 820 roubles a month at a time when the average pay of young workers was 130 roubles a month. But salaries were not the chief perquisite. There were the 'cars and special clinics, the rest homes and sanatoria, the state dachas, the trips abroad and the offices, the three-room apartments given to all Komsomol Central Committee functionaries for six months of the year. All this, including the half million roubles allocated under the 'remedial' label for strenuous work, created a powerful stimulus for lower-ranking officials of the various apparatuses to the higher apparat, it bound them more strongly than any satisfaction from telling the truth'.[22]

What was apparent in recent years was the alacrity with which the Central Committee apparatus began to acquire 'cost-accounting' centres and associations. Graivoronsky reports that between August 1989 and August 1990, it set up a score or more of subsidiary structures with staffs of nearly 500 people and foundation funds of millions of roubles. 'This is where the old Komsomol nomenklatura has shifted its employment'. The new-found economic enterprise on the part of the Komsomol led to the establishment of 'youth scientific centres', the Youth Bank, the Association of Training Co-operatives and a host of other enterprises. All of them found a guaranteed source of income from Komsomol coffers. For example, the Komsomol invested 750m roubles in the Youth Bank. 'Naturally, it is presented as yet another magnificent step in improving the lot of young people. In fact, all the profits from the Bank go to the Komsomol Central Committee; the same applies to profits from publishing activity, the commercial enterprises and membership fees paid in hard currency from foreign collective members'.[23]

As the Komsomol wound down its activities, there was a mad rush to jump on the commercial bandwagon, using Komsomol income and property for the purpose. What is interesting is the facility with which yesterday's Stalinists became today's entrepreneurs, fired by the same self-assurance that it was all for the good of Soviet youth.

A major reason for erstwhile Komsomol structures and officials turning themselves into thriving business organisations is that until 1989 Komsomol organisations, like the youth scientific centres, were practically the only institutions permitted to transfer credit into ready cash; revenues were virtually tax-exempt. It is noteworthy that the single issue that caused most heat at the April 1990 Komsomol Congress was the government proposal to raise tax on Komsomol property. It enflamed passions so much that some delegates suggested a picket of the USSR Supreme Soviet. The new tax, it was claimed, would lead to the closure of over 400,000 Komsomol enterprises.[24] The leading Party conservative Yegor Ligachov was warmly applauded at the Congress for his firm resolve to safeguard the taxation privileges enjoyed by the Komsomol.

One of the most distasteful aspects of this new-found spirit of free enterprise was the lack of scruples shown by the Komsomol businessmen in their striving for profit. It is the Komsomol that organised the first beauty contests in 1990, and that planned to stage bullfighting in Moscow's Lenin (now Central) Stadium in 1990. It is Komsomol periodicals that from 1989 began to feature scantily-clad young women in sexually provocative poses, used either to sell the periodical or products from Komsomol commercial concerns. As the weekly *Moscow News* has written 'Most of the clubs that show trashy videos round the clock are owned by the Komsomol. Most of the erotic picture exhibitions and beauty contests are run by the Komsomol economy'.[25]

A price had to be paid by the 'System' for being permitted to carry on its money-making enterprises. Graivoronsky summed it up aptly,

> 'The System must have guarantees for existing from other, more powerful Systems in the form of the State, the CPSU, the Trade Union Council, etc. A price has to be paid in loyalty. In exchange come guarantees in all manner of resolutions on strengthening Komsomol monopoly rights on economic enterprises, entry into prestigious universities and colleges, employment in certain professions (the Foreign Ministry, KGB, Diplomatic Service). In gratitude, the Komsomol agencies and leaders always observed the rules of the game, not poking their noses into politics, getting on with youth communist education as laid down by the current Party leadership. The juniors of the System assist the elders to preserve the image'.[26]

In the wake of the attempted August 1991 coup, much of Komsomol formal property (educational institutions, printing works, administrative buildings) was sequestrated by local and central government; other Komsomol enterprises swiftly switched patrons and began to operate on a self-financing basis. Thus, while the Centre for Youth Studies was shut down, the neighbouring Institute of Youth Studies (recently the Higher Komsomol School) continued its work under the Ministry of Labour. Several Komsomol functionaries moved into commercial business, while others found a home in other 'non-political' youth organisations, like the Committee on Youth Organisations.

The fortunes of two previous high-ranking Komsomol officers are of interest in this regard. In order to sell off Komsomol property, the Komsomol Central Committee created the Economic Department for Managing the Affairs of the Central Committee of the All-Union Lenin Communist Youth League or *KHOZU UD TsK VLKSM* to give it its Russian acronym. To whom did the organisation sell property and at what prices?

It sold a storehouse in Moscow's city centre (ul. P. Korchagina, dom 3) for the 'knock-down' price of 91,753 roubles and 30 dachas for some 4m roubles - although the market price of all these properties was considerably higher. The purchaser in both instances was the Russo-German Joint Venture *Burda Moden* whose Deputy Director happened to be one, Vladimir Ivanov, until recently head of *KHOZU UD TsK VLKSM* and a one-time Komsomol Central Committee member. At the same time (late 1991), the luxurious dacha on Moscow's Nikolai Hill, formerly belonging to Comrade Vladimir Zuikin, the last Komsomol chief, was acquired by the International Youth Co-operation Fund, whose President just happened to be Mr Vladimir Zuikin. As one commentator put it, 'the comrade-gentlemen are confidently continuing to build their own bright future and to consolidate external relations'.[27]

Some conclusions

In criticising the communist youth organisations, it is easy to lose sight of any positive role they have played over the years. Historically they played a part in the political socialisation of young people uprooted from the countryside and disoriented in the new urban setting. They did so by developing the values and skills appropriate to a modernising economy, by acting as a new socialising agency in a period when rapid social transformation was eroding the traditional foundations of socialisation - through the family, kinship groups, local community and religious organisations - and by attempting to shape the cultured, hard-working and honest personality who aspired to live up to the ideals of the 'New Soviet person'. In school, the youth organisations would seem to have been powerful back-up forces to teachers in encouraging diligence, discipline and selflessness, which were probably more effective coming from the peer group itself rather than being directly imposed by adults.

The Komsomol may have integrated some young people into the building of a socialist society; however, it clearly estranged others through excessive bureaucracy, discipline, routine and invasions of personal lifestyles. Times were changing and the Komsomol was too slow to adapt; it was hard to maintain revolutionary enthusiasm among boys and girls born in the 1970s and 1980s. Nor was it easy to bring up young people in what they perceived as old-fashioned, parochial values at a time when increasing exposure to Western youth culture and the mounting restlessness of urban teenagers were leading to a polarisation of values between the younger and older generations. Established youth organisations and the Churches have encountered similar problems in the West.

One of the inevitable consequences of the Komsomol being the only permitted youth organisation of the only permitted party in power was the spawning within it of bandwagon careerists, corrupt officials, political 'radishes' (red on the outside, white on the inside) who paid lip service to communism and concern for young people, while enjoying their *frais de representation*: trips abroad, chauffeur-driven limousines, special (closed to the public) shops, hospitals, dachas, rest homes, their high salaries augmented by their tax-free 'packet', their private film screenings, their booked seats in top theatres for performances that excluded the public, and the rest.

Such a blatant abuse of privileges, the dividends of political rank, helped create a bureaucracy of privileged Komsomol functionaries divorced from the mass of young people, intent on preserving their own position. Such bureaucrats rose to power, moreover, not by the will and demands of those beneath them, but by appointment from above, from Party officials on whom they were entirely dependent.

This system of privileges had long since destroyed any popular belief that young people were masters of their own destiny and country. It blunted the feeling of responsibility for what happened around them, it created a 'them versus us' syndrome when 'they' enjoy prequisites gained not from owning property or from class exploitation, but from *control* over the fruits of others' labour, from privileges abrogated by the ruling party and its youth wing. 'We' respond in varying degrees of passive resignation and, in recent years, active resistance, partly motivated by disillusionment with insincere moralisers and cynical careerists. It is clearly not going to be easy, in view of the legacy left by past politicians, to convince young people that future political leaders who speak in their name are making genuine attempts to establish honest values, integrity and patriotism.

Young people need to feel trusted: to write, dance, sing, study, travel without having to prove their political loyalty. That is what the Komsomol and Party leaders failed to grasp; they eventually paid the price of their own duplicity and isolation from young people.

Notes

1 *Vsesoyuzyny Leninsky kommunistichesky soyuz molodoyzni. Naglyadnoye posobie* (Moscow, 1985), p. 39; *Molodoi Kommunist* 1987, no. 3, p. 9.

2 *Organizatsionno-ustavnye voprosy komsomolskoi raboty* (Moscow, 1973), p. 59.

3 See *Argumenty i Fakty* March 1991, no. 12, p. 8: the figures are estimated to the end of the year.

4 Betsy McKay, 'Communists meet to reform party youth wing', *Moscow Times* 21 April 1992, p. 1 and p. 4. Delegates vowed to teach youth the principles of Marxism-Leninism and to restore a united, multi-national state - the USSR.

5 See N. Popov, 'Krizis doveriya - krizis vlasti', *Ogonek* 1990, no. 7, p. 3; *Argumenty i Fakty* 1990, no. 7, p. 6; *Dossier 'Vybory-90'* (Moscow, 1990), p. 7.

6 *Materialy XXI-ovo syezda VLKSM* (Moscow, 1990), p. 194.

7 *Pervy vserossisky syezd RKSM* (3rd ed, Moscow-Leningrad, 1926), p. 98.

8 Ibid, pp. 97-98.

9 See Ralph Fisher, *Pattern for Soviet Youth. A Study of the Congresses of the Komsomol, 1918-54* (New York, Columbia University Press, 1959). p. 28. Party membership at the time of the Third Komsomol Congress was 600,000: see *Tretiy vserossisky syezd rossisyskovo kommunisticheskovo soyuza molodozhi* (Moscow-Leningrad, 1926), p. 28.

10   *VII syezd Vsesoyoznovo Leniniskovo soyuza molodozhi* (Moscow-Leningrad, 1926), p. 193.

11   *VKP (b) o komsomole i molodyozhi. Sbornik resheniy i postanovleniy partii o molodyozhi* (Moscow, 1938), p. 77

12   V.I. Lenin, 'Internatsional molodyozhi', *Polnoye sobranie sochinenii* vol. 30 (Moscow, 1975), p. 226. The quotation was suppressed from general publication until the Komsomol weekly *Sobesednik* printed it, without comment, in August 1987, No. 33, p. 3.

13   M.S. Gorbachov, *Molodyozh - tvorcheskaya sila revolutsionnovo obnovleniya* (Moscow, 1989), p. 31.

14   M.S. Gorbachov, 'Otkrovenny razgovor s delegatami syezda', *Komsomolskaya Pravda* 12 April 1990, p. 2.

15   See *Komsomolskaya pravda* 3 August 1989.

16   Ibid.

17   *O Polozhenii v Komsomole i o putakh yevo vykhoda iz krizisa* (Moscow, 1990), p. 37.

18   I. Solganik, 'Syezd komsomola: vzglyad iz koridora', *Argumenty i Fakty* 1990, No. 16, p. 5.

19   Maria Pastukhova, 'Dengi my otrabatyvayem', *Sobesednik* 1990, No. 6, p. 3.

20   S. Anokhin et al, *Ocherednoi krizis ili tupik (polemicheskie zametki o komsomole)* (Moscow, 1989), p. 1.

21   V. Graivoronsky, 'Kuda letyat milliony,' *Moskovsky komsomolets* 13 April 1990, p. 1.

22   Ibid.

23   Ibid.

24   'Trudnosti s parliamentom,' *Moskovsky komsomolets* 13 April 1990, p. 1.

25   Yelena Tokareva, 'XXI syezd komsomola,' *Moskovskie novosti* 1990, No. 16, p. 4.

26   Graivoronsky 1990 op cit.

27   'Komsomolskaya 'Burda',' *Argumenty i Fakty* January 1992, p. 2.

7 The spiritual and cultural values of young people in a post-Totalitarian state

IGOR ILYNSKY

Introduction

The downfall of the totalitarian system resulted in a crumbling of the system of spiritual, moral and cultural values that had cemented the evidently monolithic blocs of the social edifice; they were in varying degrees part of the inner world of human beings designated as 'the Soviet people'. Inasmuch as new values have not yet emerged with specific, real and practical meaning for Russian people, *a crisis of values* has arisen.

The former communist ideal of social development has come crashing down; it had provided the backbone of official ideology, had permeated the whole system of state education, socialisation, propaganda and, therefore, again in varying degrees, of the consciousness of millions of people. Yet the demise of one social ideal has not led to the emergence of another, new ideal which might enjoy public trust and attract the public. Spokespersons for 'radical' democracy have not yet been able seriously to substantiate a constructive idea of prospects for social development which today could be recognised as consolidating society. There is an exceedingly vague conception in most people's minds about a society with a solid market economy and high standard of living; for the moment this conception plays the part of an ideal. As a consequence, we now have a crisis of *spiritual* and, above all, of spiritual-theoretical values that has been brewing for many years.

Spirituality

The status of *spirituality itself*, accumulating within itself all supreme human values, has diminished in the hierarchy of values. Sociological surveys undertaken in 1987-88 show that 26 per cent of young people put *material* provision among the highest values, while a 1990 survey indicates a rise to 42 per cent and a 1991 survey up to 58 per cent. That happened even before price liberalisation. In the hierarchy of everyday values, material provision rose from eighth place in 1989 to third by 1991 (only love and family happiness, and health stand higher). The share of young people who put spirituality among the highest values fell from 16.2 per cent (14th place) to 11.7 per cent (18th place). So we can see that young people's weak hold on spirituality has grown even feebler; this continued in 1992-3.

Almost 37 per cent of those surveyed believe that society's transition to a market economy is eroding still further society's spiritual reference points. A mere 23.8 per cent hold the view that this transition is likely to create favourable conditions for society's spiritual recuperation. Some 40 per cent have no set view or simply have given no thought to the potential effect of market relations on society's spiritual life. More than two-thirds do not include spirituality in the virtues needed for young people during the transition to the market; virtually 44 per cent of young people associate the transition with a lower spiritual-moral protection; 27.6 per cent are concerned with counteracting the aggression inherent in lack of spirituality. The proportion of young people who feel that Russians need spirituality during the transition period comprise less than 28 per cent (some 15 per cent of those surveyed believe that they themselves possess that virtue). The problems of material provision and survival increasingly press back young people's spiritual requirements and needs.

Freedom

Youngsters have a poor understanding of the sense of *freedom as a spiritual value* (for the moment just about the only real gain from perestroika and reform); they ill appreciate that the employment of freedom presupposes individual spirituality, otherwise it turns into wilfulness which violates freedom and the interests of those around one. The majority of young people underestimate the truth that freedom has a correlation with rights and the law, that the law is a measure of freedom, that freedom itself is law-governed and determined on the basis of moderation. During the 1987-88 sociological survey, fewer than 20 per cent of young people put legal guarantees of freedom among the highest values; the figures for 1990 and 1991 were 26 per cent and about 25 per cent. As many as 42 per cent of young boys and girls explained that a necessary condition of freedom for each person was understanding and realisation by them and other people of the principle of unity of civil rights and duties. A sense of responsibility is present only in a relatively small number of young people. According to our 1990 survey, only some 15 per cent of young people were focused on the self-development of social responsibility; that number had declined to 8.6 per cent in 1991. Out of young entrepreneurs surveyed in August 1992, only 11.5 per cent pronounced themselves capable of taking responsibility upon themselves (although 42.6 per cent recognised the significance of that quality). Hence the legal nihilism and lack of responsibility of young people in all its forms and manifestations.

Social justice

Evaluation of the actual state of *social justice* is worsening as a high spiritual value. Surveys carried out by the Sociology Institute of the Russian Academy of Sciences and other institutions indicate that, while in 1988 some 26 per cent of those questioned had not encountered injustice, in 1990 the figure was only 13.4 per cent. The proportion of those who had *never* met it fell from 32 per cent to 23.3 per cent. On the other hand, the number of those frequently encountering injustice jumped from 36.8 per cent to 59.6 per cent. According to a survey carried out by the Youth Research Centre in 1991, about 30 per cent of young people experienced fear when confronted with injustice. There is a clear tendency to devalue justice as a value. In the course of the 1987-88 survey, some 27 per cent of students and young workers put social justice as one of the top values; by 1990, the percentage had fallen to 22.3 per cent; while in 1991 it was 19.2 per cent (8th, 10th and 15th places respectively among over 20 everyday values). The trend towards a weaker orientation of young people on social justice is patently obvious. While in 1987-88, more than 41 per cent of young people regarded fulfilment of social justice principles as their own personal goal (first place among basic personal objectives), by 1990 it had fallen to 33.5 per cent (third place) and by 1991 to 19.3 per cent (fifth place).

Lack of faith

A *lack of faith* in anything or anyone is acquiring blanket coverage. Today, 44 per cent of young people in Russia think that their generation is one without ideals; 43 per cent are depressed about the uncertain future. Disillusionment with past and present, pessimism about the future and loss of vital reference points have all become mass phenomena. In excess of three quarters of young people have a sense of dissatisfaction with life, a lack of confidence in the future; they adversely assess the aims and paths of development of contemporary society (only 5-10 per cent may be called optimists). And virtually two-thirds regard themselves as being socially exposed.

Fear of the future

In the last couple of years sociologists have noted a rapid rise (roughly doubling each year) in *fear of the future*: according to a survey of February 1993, as many as 24.3 per cent out of 1,037 young people questioned stated their fear of the future. Among specific fears, they indicated ethnic war in first place (34.5 per cent); followed by loneliness (31.3 per cent), poverty (28.3 per cent), illness (27.4 per cent), banditry (22.4 per cent), loss of employment (18.3 per cent) and hunger (16.3 per cent). Fears of that nature are in many ways novel for Russian youngsters and therefore paralyse the will of a substantial number. At the same time, there is a noticeable blunting of fear, people are growing accustomed to it and converting it into a constant background characteristic of the new social situation, into a powerful stimulus of self-development and of social activity. Undoubtedly, however, there are negative consequences of fear for people's health and attitude to life and those around them, as well as for the whole atmosphere of public life.

The role of the individual

What we are witnessing is an active redistribution within the structure and hierarchy of youth value orientations in Russia. In the eyes of young people *the role and meaning of the individual* as an active, independent person is markedly changing. At the same time, there is a growth also in people's understanding of themselves as a value in itself. A posing of the question of human rights and freedoms and the protection of personal honour and dignity have shifted from mere propaganda to the practical plane. The human personality is moving to the centre of the new world outlook and that is an important earnest of success in shaping the new society. Only 13 per cent expect state assistance if they fall on hard times, while as many as 50 per cent of their parents expect it and 20 per cent of their friends. Young people appreciate with increasing lucidity that they can rely only on themselves in realising their life plans and attaining success in life today (71 per cent). At the same time, we may note a sharp decline in the importance of such highly-placed values as being of use to society, being needed by people, and just as marked a rise in the share of so-called private, individual values. Today, 70 per cent of young people believe that they can rely only on themselves, need to think only of themselves and their own affairs. The first few places among significant values go to health, family, living conditions, material provision, health of children, loyal friends - i.e. general human values. On the whole, this is a healthy trend. But individualisation as the antithesis of extreme collectivism has patently overstepped the mark. Young people are capable of harmonising their own common aspirations, of self-regulation (which would conform to their own interests) and, as a result, come into conflict with society in many areas. Values that constitute primarily the goals of human life (cognition, education, work, creative endeavour, science, literature and the arts, culture generally) have sharply diminished in importance, moved into the lower part of values on the hierarchical scale, have become value-means instead of value-goals. Thus, together with a diminished value in service by super-individual goals, there is a simplification and primitivisation of genuinely essential values, depriving them of the spiritual, enhancing principle. Yet the lower the importance of values that people serve and for which they live, the lower is individual worth. The pragmatism which most of modern youth espouses actually leads to a growth of selfishness, cynicism, extremism and aggressiveness.

Human life

The *value of human life* has noticeably fallen in the scale of values. The mounting number of murders is proof enough of that. Some 6 per cent of young people admit to considering murder if they were to be paid for it, according to 1991-92 surveys. There is an increase in the number of suicides, attempted suicide and violence against the individual. As many as 56 per cent of young people questioned accept the use of violence against the individual in order to prove they are in the right and to attain their own ends. At the same time, two thirds of those surveyed in various age categories claim that human life has no value. Out of the host of vital problems young people have begun increasingly to advance that of personal security (every fourth school pupil and young worker and every fifth student). Youngsters want to own a personal weapon and call for the establishment of professional security services in schools and colleges. It is of great urgency for young minds to believe in the essential self-value of the individual and, at the same time, to have an understanding of how life has meaning if it is concerned not simply with self-gratification, but also with serving ultra-individual objectives: one's country, society, the community, art, science, etc.

Religion

The freedom of philosophical views and faiths, as well as a spiritual vacuum in society, have led to a substantial growth in religiosity. The number of those convinced that only faith in God will help humankind to be moral has risen from 20 per cent to 49 per cent - of whom one in ten is firmly convinced in the veracity of this thesis. We can denote a minimum of three categories in regard to religion:

(i)   young people for whom religion is a system-forming entire value structure (the 'believers' - 10 per cent);

(ii) those for whom religion exerts a marked influence on their structure of values - 20 per cent; and

(iii) the non-believers (atheists) - about 60 per cent - who experience no religious feelings at all.

The rise in religiosity has a stable correlation with the demise of communist ideology; it is also related to two other factors: first, a special refinement or 'artistic portrayal' of nature and second, a sense of being merely a grain of sand in a world of tempests and catastrophes (*Sturm und Drang*).

The latter group accounts for the socially defenceless, lost, prospect-less souls who have received a religious upbringing (mainly in the family). The stratum of militant believers among young people in general is fairly small and has no serious impact on the mass of youth. Strong natures do not normally have a need for religion ('A strong person is his/her own God').

Belief in the potential of science

Young people's loss of social ideals, their shift from social and collective life into introspection, the circumstance of disillusionment and the undermining of all and everything is helping to fill minds with mystical content, superstition and lack of faith in the potential of science. Research of recent years shows that 80 per cent of young people are today interested in arcane phenomena (telepathy, bipolar experiences, extra-terrestrial phenomena, etc.). Approximately 60 per cent believe that far from all phenomena existing in nature may be explained by means of science. One in ten young people (one in five students of the humanities) are convinced that phenomena exist which lie beyond the bounds of science, even the most refined scientific spheres. One in five young people claim that they have directly encountered mysterious phenomena in their lives, including sightings of unidentified flying objects - some have even had dealings with extra-terrestrial beings.

As many as 34 per cent of St. Petersburg and 27 per cent of Leningrad Region residents believe in astrology, 33 per cent and 36 per cent respectively in the evil eye, 20 per cent and 21 per cent believe in the imminent arrival of people from outer space and 8 per cent and 10 per cent respectively in 'magic'. The picture is similar in other parts of Russia. Sociological research into the state of the book market confirms the irrational nature of young people's spiritual world. More than half of all readers are today interested in books on UFO's, extra-terrestrial beings, ways and means of self-improvement, meditation, spiritualism, werewolves and sorcery. This type of literature takes fourth place after detective stories, science fiction, historical and adventure books. It is by no means merely a harmless pastime, in so far as the majority of such people represent ready material for manipulation of mind and behaviour. The behaviour of millions of people was inexplicable (irrational) when they first read in the newspapers about death demands for 'enemies of the people'; on occasion, people had even demanded death for themselves even though they knew they were completely innocent.

A crisis of spiritual-*moral values* has burst upon Russian society. The socialist, class morality has fallen by the wayside, while a new type of morality and moral values based on general human values has not come into existence. The boundaries between good and bad, right and wrong are now worn away. The strong reinforcing of property differentiation, the need to survive and fight for an elementary standard of living have established prerequisites for the spontaneous formation of a 'new' set of mores behind which is the philosophy of crude pragmatism, perverted individualism. As a result, we have a situation of moral permissiveness, a 'no holds barred' morality, when the person with more rights is always right, when might is right, when the more cunning and devious person is right, when those without moral principles live better than others.

Individualism

Individualistic morality is rapidly being affirmed in the minds of a substantial part of young people. We may assess the scale of this process from the following facts. Only a little over 8 per cent of young people can today count on help from their own group if needed. The overwhelming majority (more than 52 per cent) can count on their parents to help them out in awkward situations. One in three can rely only on themselves. In evaluating the state of mutual relationships on an individual basis, 71 per cent of young men and women believe that nowadays people are less willing to aid one another than a few years ago, 62 per cent firmly believe that morality is diminishing and people relate less humanely to one another. Every other person is certain that among those around them the great bulk are occupied solely with themselves and attaining personal satisfaction. A mere 6 per cent feel that those they come into contact with possess the virtue of honesty, while fewer than 8 per cent note a sense of justice in their nearest and dearest.

There is a very rapid re-orientation of young people's moral awareness in regard to things which only yesterday were categorically condemned - sexual dissolution, prostitution, drugs, homosexuality, thieving. Such things no longer excite moral condemnation; in fact, most young people are more inclined to justify those who go in for prostitution, drug addiction and crime. A substantial part of young men and women are inclined to treat past cruelty towards such behaviour merely as an element of the old lack of freedom inherent in totalitarian society.

Cultural values

Russian society is facing a crisis of *spiritual-aesthetic values*, a crisis of national culture. While the culture of socialist realism is being ridiculed, there is no sign of the emergence of a new stratum of philosophers, scholars, writers, poets, playwrights, musicians and artists who would be the people's spiritual leaders. The culture of a nation - continuing the best traditions of the past - has fallen apart. Cultural development is largely focused on works concerned with the distant Russian past or with foreign, mainly American genres.

The inculcation of market relations into the cultural sphere has had huge negative consequences for young people. We have destroyed the *infra-structure of culture*, as well as virtually the entire network of children's libraries, youth cinemas, theatres, clubs and libraries, the system of sport and recreation for casual enthusiasts, youth tourism within the country, youth publishers, youth newspapers and magazines, youth radio and TV programmes. This means the practical extinction of all channels through which producers and authors could communicate cultural values to their customers - youth. We have a sharp contradiction in the sphere of professional and amateur creative activity, in particular the hundreds and thousands of amateur art, music, drama and other clubs and, with them, the producers of spiritual values, the mass of cultural values themselves. Millions of talented young people are now deprived of conditions for creative endeavour, for self-fulfilment in terms of creativity. Those who are particularly suffering are youngsters in the countryside and provincial towns where cultural life has practically ceased to exist or been confined to the TV screen - if one exists. The frequent hiking of cinema and theatre ticket prices has put them out of reach of a large number of young people. Among the common leisure activities of young people, only 9.8 per cent of those surveyed name visits to the theatre, museums and exhibitions, and fewer than 4 per cent mention participation in any form of artistic endeavour. There can be no doubt that we are witnessing the alienation of the great bulk of youth from the values of world and Russian culture; they are becoming culture-less, since spiritual freedom is unthinkable without its manifestation in artistic behaviour and cultural development. Creativity involves spirituality, the free 'play' of the imagination and emotions, it is incompatible with routine and inertia. Some 85 per cent of young Russians recognise the decline in culture, as do 96 per cent of young creative workers. More than 44 per cent of creative workers fear that transition to the market will have further problems for cultural development and only 17.5 per cent express hopes for a cultural renaissance associated with the transition.

Youth culture

We now see a marked boundary between the emergent elite and *mass* culture oriented not on individual development, but on its diversion. Big changes are occurring in *youth sub-culture* which had previously been essentially a *counter-culture* standing opposed to official culture. Today, music and song, poetry and painting, the studio theatrical movement and cinematography have all lost their civic content and critical pathos which had been so attractive to the awakening mass youth consciousness; they no longer express the interests and needs of most youngsters. This is particularly apparent in the fate of rock music where groups which had only recently occupied a high place on the ranking scale of youth musical preferences have slipped to the bottom. They have been replaced by rock music of quite a different genre - blatantly pessimistic and apocalyptic. Another direction taken by contemporary rock music is commercial rock which increasingly fuses with pop music designed to gratify the very undemanding needs of some young teenagers. Something similar is happening with 'youth' cinema, painting and theatre.

Leisure activity

Practically the only channel for the wide access of the great bulk of young people to artistic values of both world and Russian culture is now television, and partly the cassette recorder. That has swiftly made itself felt in the structure of *young people's spare time*; passive forms of leisure now predominate. On average, some 76 per cent of young people more often spend their free time in front of the TV or in the company of friends listening almost exclusively to pop music. At the same time, only one in ten (according to their own self-evaluation) prefer to spend what remains of their spare time on going to studio clubs, one in 16 on self-education, and one in six on sport. There is a marked rise in 'domestication' of the consumption of cultural values and a reduction in the number of channels through which a young person comes into contact with the world of art, literature and painting; we can expect in the not-so-distant future that Russia will find itself in the situation depicted by Ray Bradbury in his science fiction story *436° Fahrenheit*, where the heroine socialises with the exclusively 'TV relatives' and has no wish to have contact with real live people.

There exists an obvious danger of 'Americanisation' of young minds; it is a danger that is still only dimly perceived even by those who determine cultural policy, at a time when practically every European culture has had for several decades effective laws that prevent American 'cultural' products from flooding the national market. From the mid-1960s, for example, France has had a law setting quotas on American films shown in both state and private cinemas. If American films exceed French films (according to the law, the correlation must be no higher than 51 per cent to 49 per cent, French to US) a fine is incurred as well as loss of licence. A whole set of protectionist measures exists in Spain, the Netherlands, Italy and Germany. There can be little doubt that Russia too needs a purposeful policy against excessive penetration of American mass culture.

Generational conflict

The crisis of spiritual-theoretical, moral and aesthetic values has engendered in Russian society a most crude *generation conflict* which is not confined to the 'fathers and sons' differences of opinion on dress and hairstyle, tastes in music, dance and behaviour style - immanent in all societies and at all times; this generation conflict affects philosophical, spiritual and attitudinal principles of social and human development, basic views on economics and production, on society's material life. The older generation finds itself in a position where the material and spiritual legacy which, by laws of continuity, it should and is obliged to pass on to its successors is, to all intents and purposes, absent. The social values by which the older generation has lived have largely lost all meaning and practical significance in the new historical situation, and therefore cannot be passed on to the younger generation, inasmuch as they are unsuitable for both the present and the future. Russian society is actually facing not so much a conflict as a *break in generations* reflecting a rupture in continuity, a rupture in historical development, a transition of society to a principally different economic, social and political system.

The younger generation has found itself in an awkward, different and most complex situation where it is destined by the logic of history to *continue* development on the basis of inherited material and spiritual values; it is obliged, while being at an emergent stage, to take part in working out those values, mostly having to do that work independently, often in the face of the old thinking of their parents and of their attempts to restore the old values.

Depending on the level of their development, young people vary greatly in their assessment of the times in which they live (1992): 73 per cent in all categories regard it as 'confused' and 'aggressive' in which 'one has to grab all one can', a 'time of loss and disillusionment, destruction of society'; 30.5

per cent assess it as a time for urgent action to save Russia; and only 10 per cent regard it as a time of good prospects and hope. Social awareness seems to be formulating a stereotype of Russia's age-old backwardness and its people's primitiveness. The values of Russian science, education and culture are being reduced to naught in the public mind. As many as 48 per cent of Russian students feel that the great history of the Russian people is all in the past, while the future is problematic in the extreme.

Young people's assessment of their own generation is just as contradictory. Students at six leading St. Petersburg universities and institutes were asked 'With what of the following assessments of the present younger generation would you agree?'. The following responses (in percentages) were obtained:

Table 7.1
Assessments of the younger generation, St. Petersburg, Russia, 1993

Answers to the question: With which of the following assessments of the present younger generation would you agree?

Generation that is:	Yes	Partly	No	±	'Yes' or partly 'Yes'
Sceptical	35.4	51.9	12.7	1.77	87.3
Aggressive	37.4	49.5	13.1	2.45	86.9
Cynical	24.7	57.8	17.5	1.93	82.5
Pragmatic	26.3	52.3	21.4	1.95	78.6
Disillusioned	26.8	47.8	25.4	1.99	74.6
Hopeful	22.7	49.0	28.3	2.06	71.7
Deceived	32.3	39.2	28.5	1.96	71.5
Frightened	15.2	37.2	47.3	2.32	52.7
Lost	10.3	34.3	55.4	1.76	44.6
Reconciled	7.4	35.7	56.8	2.49	43.1
Hard to say	62.4	26.2	11.5	1.49	88.6

The picture changes radically when young people make a self-evaluation. To the question 'To what generation would you associate yourself?', the same students responded as shown in Table 7.2.

Despite the overall tension and evident state of conflict between generations, what is striking is the reserve with which 'children' relate to their 'parents'. To the question 'Do you agree that the older generation is responsible for all the misfortunes suffered by our country?' (posed in February 1993), only 7.3 per cent answered 'yes, fully agree'; 42.7 per cent said they 'partly agreed'; 32.5 per cent did 'not agree' and 12 per cent found it hard to say.

Table 7.2
Young people's self-evaluation in Russia

Answers to the question: To what generation would you associate yourself?

Answer	*Percentage*
Sceptical	13.5
Aggressive	1.0
Cynical	1.5
Pragmatic	7.7
Disillusioned	9.7
Hopeful	20.3
Deceived	4.4
Frightened	2.9
Lost	2.7
Reconciled	3.9
No response	32.3

When asked 'How do you relate to the older generation?', 1.6 per cent said 'with admiration', 36.1 per cent 'with respect', 30.3 per cent 'with sympathy', 17.6 per cent ' with lack of understanding', 3 per cent 'with contempt', 0.8 per cent 'with hatred', while 13.2 per cent found it difficult to respond. Moreover, 44.2 per cent assessed their relations with parents as good, 15.4 per cent as bearable and only 3 per cent as 'scandalous'.

Old versus new values

In so far as the old values have not vanished altogether from the minds of young people, while new values have not yet taken root, the one often cohabits the other; we may single out a few typological groups *whose representatives exhibit a similar psychological and behavioural reaction to the changing social situation.*

The *first group* includes people *preserving former values.* Recognition of the fact that their values have lost their dominant status may produce different reactions. There may be an attempt to defend these values, having maintained self-identification of the former type. This is most strikingly demonstrated in the various societies and associations of the *Yedinstvo* (Unity), 'Party of Proletarian Dictatorship', 'Communist Initiative' or Communist Youth League types. But there evidently also exists a fairly broad social spectrum that retains these values in an 'encapsulated' form. Preservation of old values at a time when they have changed from being socially approved to 'rejected and despised' presents a certain danger to such people and therefore may be accompanied by aggression or, on the contrary, a stupor-like depressive reaction. There may be a political battle for the erstwhile value norms accompanied by political exaltation and even suicide. For most people in this category there is a typical social mimicry and external adaptation to the new values, yet a dumb resistance to them and a belief in the possible return to the old values as dominant once more. Such people may be far more numerous than is 'manifest'.

Representatives of this group are express bearers of an authoritarian cast of mind for whom a 'flight from freedom' is typical, a belief in the possibility of single social choice, in a charismatic leader who 'knows what's needed'. For objective reasons a relatively small number of young people come into this category. They are either under 18 or over 28 years of age. Such age characteristics merit more careful examination. It may be connected with various circumstances. Young boys and girls under 18 have grown up in the difficult years of perestroika's social experiments, accompanied on an everyday level more with losses than gains. The proclaimed new values are not yet internalised by some of them as a possible point of reference. It is possible that this group of young people shares the values of its immediate environment, especially the family. On the other hand, more mature young people (28 years and over) who belong to this group already perceive the 'stagnation' period society as a model of social stability and economic well-being. Why is this so? Probably, it is not simply because the overall socio-economic and political situation is complex and unstable, but also because this group of young people is less protected by the older generation of their family and has to tackle new vital problems independently. They retain an orientation on former, now non-functional means, an inertia of a life path travelled according to a 'Soviet' scenario. This group would seem from our research to account for some 7-10 per cent of respondents - 19 per cent among adults.

The *second group* includes people who are also aware of the crumbling of old values but, in contrast with the first group, exhibit not an encapsulation of old values, but their correction while retaining the value nucleus (here referring to a single state and the basic principles of social structure). Their logic is approximately as follows: 'The initial values were distorted, but one ought not to reject them, all we need to do is correct them'. People in this group are quite self-critical. They believe in the possibility of change for the better on the basis of adapting old values to the new situation. Their state of mind may be described as liberal-reformist, but only to a certain degree: if a market, then it must be regulated; if property, then it should be collective (in terms of production), etc. The group is represented in society by certain strains of the labour movement and is likely to be located more on the periphery than in the centre (Moscow, St. Petersburg). It is also possible that the value orientations of this group are popular with part of the armed forces and the technical intelligentsia. In age, they are about 27-30 years old. The group may well grow in step with increasing economic crisis and the lack of a socially unifying ideology capable of replacing the old one; if this happens the significance of the 'nucleus' will become intensified. For the time being, the number of young people whom our research shows fall into this second category amounts to 23 per cent of those surveyed - 32 per cent of adults.

The *third group* embraces those exhibiting a 'radical-illusory recon-struction of values'; more simply, they have turned things on their head. Typically they hate the 'old world', are intolerant of all other value orientations apart from their own; and they are aggressive. One may define this type of thinking as quasi-revolutionary. Such people aspire to sunder all links with the old structures, to destroy them completely. Their social criticism is nihilistic and destructive, although in words they aspire to introduce new forms of life, new socio-political structures. In deeds, however, they exhibit a desire to destroy and repress their ideological and political opponents, thereby reproducing the 'image of the enemy' and other stereotypes of thinking critical of the first group, particularly the search for a version of the 'bright future', but this time a capitalist one for which one may once more 'change' history and clear a way for the new society. Such thinking may be described as 'mirroring' the first type. Here, once more, the common people act as the building material, suitable or unsuitable for the new version of the 'bright future'. And the unsuitable human material may at best find themselves, at the will of these builders, as 'isolated from society'; yet they also may be pitilessly crushed in the course of subsequent social experimenting. The thinking of such people utterly lacks historical continuity; it is collectively based on a reference group and everything outside perceived in an exceedingly intolerant way. This is Bolshevism stood on its head. It may have nationalistic embellishments and be elevated to the level of national chauvinism. Unfortunately, this type of con- sciousness is vividly apparent today in the works of several journalists, publicists, parliamentarians, part of the technical intelligentsia and members of the national movements. Our research pinpoints a group of young people aged 21-27 years, 23 per cent of the total surveyed who may be classified in this way.

The *fourth group* is another type of over-estimation of values; it may be designated as the realist-radical. Its position does not renounce the former historical and cultural experience and does not share the aspirations of destructive radicalism no matter whether it calls itself 'democratic' or 'patriotic'. The group's thinking bears and seeks real possibilities for constructive action on the basis of new values. At the same time, it is historical inasmuch as, instead of primitive, simplistic-radical programmes, it focuses on the complicated and contradictory, though objective picture of the world. It really does recognise and appreciate individual rights as having priority over group, collective, national, regional or other rights. The priority of individual rights is a form of litmus test for realising genuine democracy. That is why one cannot regard many of the national movements as democratic. What is typical of the fourth group is a greater predilection for the historicity of thinking, toleration, an ability for social adaptation in the new circumstances. Such a synthesising of values would appear to be the most fruitful of all. Our research indicates that some 30 per cent of young people and 20 per cent of adults fall into this group.

The *fifth group* embraces those for whom the crisis of values is expressed in their complete and utter destruction. The entire field of individual activity is disappearing, making any action futile. In terms of behavioural attitudes, members of this group react differently: in stupor, in humility, in all forms of absenteeism - emigration, going 'underground', alcoholism, drug addiction, asocial behaviour, suicide. Such thinking is, in practice, unstructured and marginal. The group may include lumpen proletarians, as well as old age pensioners and, of course, the young. There is a risk of anyone joining the group if the present crumbling of social relations continues. Elements of frustrated thinking according to this type are apparent in all groups; in pure form it would seem to account for 5 per cent of young people and 7 per cent of adults.

Legitimacy in acknowledgement of violence is a definite characteristic in four of the five groups (numbers 1-3 and 5) - that is, for the overwhelming majority. These young people are oriented both on subordination to coercive forms of influence, and to the use of such forms in relation to other members of society, up to and including the extreme 'isolating from society' of members of those social groups that may be 'socially dangerous'. Within their consciousness there is an intensive presence of 'an image of the enemy'. Such 'enemies' include 'communists', 'democrats', 'immigrant workers', 'separatists', other 'ethnic groups'. Thus, practically any social group may be included in the 'socially dangerous' category liable to strong-arm measures depending on the situation.

The thinking of members of the typological groups 1-3 and 5 possesses a weakly expressed subjectivity; it is predominantly irrational and susceptible to manipulation. Group identification takes priority over individual identification. This combination is a characteristic of the thinking and state of the 'value field' which shows that there exists a real possibility of support from most people for strong-arm methods of reform, as well as an 'iron-fist' policy.

Features of the youth socio-psychological portrait have become far more exaggerated owing to the very profound social changes taking place against the background of the exacerbating economic crisis and political instability in Russia, which has sharply narrowed possibilities for self-determination and worsened the social position in which young people have to live. We note an acute and variegated stratification of young people into rich and poor, native residents and migrants, 'ours' and 'theirs', the elite and the plebs, the lucky and the rejected, leaders and outsiders, democrats and totalitarians, etc.

Parallels with the 1920s?

All that is very similar to events in Russia in the mid-1920s. At that time many were certain that outside the country, behind the 'turn of events', lay world revolution and communist society. Then, all of a sudden, they had instead NEP - the New Economic Policy, a deep-going socio-material stratification and restoration of the overthrown classes. As a result, substantial sections of youth fell into apathy, drunkenness, hooliganism and sexual depravity. History is repeating itself with the only difference the youth of the 1920s were overwhelmingly a generation of victorious revolution, possessing a powerful charge and therefore ready to bear anything in order to make yet another 'last and decisive' leap into the new world.

Their contemporary equivalents have never conquered anyone. The system came crashing down all by itself. Finding themselves in homeostasis, with few exceptions, they were in no way prepared for the 'last', 'first' or any kind of struggle, being used to waiting merely for the longed-for blessings promised by ideologists of perestroika to fall from the sky. That explains the passive-survival position of the bulk of youth in regard to the current reforms.

A loss of direction?

A study of the political stereotypes of youth, its perceptions of the personages, objectives and content of power, the ways and means and results of implementation of power, as well as of participation in the political affairs of society, demonstrate that we must cast aside all ideas formed in the perestroika years concerning an identically democratic orientation of young people. The political thinking of most young people is distinguished rather by a pendulum transitoriness (swinging one way, then the other), than by being shaped by new values of pluralist democracy. The political thinking and social opinion of young people in today's conditions of radical reform show an increasing neo-conservative syndrome (one in three hanker after the 'strong hand'), as well as right- and left-wing radicalism; the centrist orientation is steadily being eroded. An important feature of youth's political thinking is its increasingly weak, almost disappearing, Bolshevist characteristic and, provisionally and unevenly, according to the various youth groups, its weakening imperialist ideology. The practical absence of any orientation on a worthwhile ideology is particularly striking. What is marked is a tendency to increasing political indifference (only one in ten is ready and able to display political activity - and that only in extreme circumstances). Very small groups of politically active young people look to the new parties and social movements. The ecological movements, various charitable organisations and philanthropic funds have most sympathisers among the youth.

Conclusions

A worsening of the overall situation is not only restraining any spiritual emergence of young people, it is having a deforming impact on the whole process. There is a marked weakening among young people of any orientation on spiritual values and strengthening of the process of soul-lessness which threatens youth's spiritual development and, therefore, the spiritual recovery of society as well.

A further deepening of the crisis is likely to have an even more destructive effect on the value world of present and future generations. The most profound effect will be the loss to the value world of that part of youth which has the weakest links with the family, is quite backward in its social development and least successful in education ('children of the street') - up to 50 per cent of all young people.

The current generation of young people may overwhelmingly be described as marginal; it has not mastered the values of the 'old' world; yet it has no opportunity to internalise the values of the 'new' world in any serious way. Hence the contradictory nature of the value world (and behaviour) both in terms of the group and the individual.

The present generation of youth is virtually free of the influence of communist ideology; all the same, levelling tendencies are noticeable quite strongly in its value orientations.

The value structure of youth is marked by a sharp reinforcement within it of individual values: family, love, personal success, material provision, comfort, etc. These are changes that appear to be stable.

The rapid growth in national (and nationalist) factors is having an impact on youth value structures. The rise in the 'wounded' national self-awareness of the Russian people and Russian youth is becoming decisive. Which direction the development will take is bound to depend on how well the governing structures manage to deal with the trend. What is certain is that it is impossible now to hold it back or stifle it.

In the event of unpropititious economic development, there is the possibility of a 'fusing' of economic, political and nationalist factors with clearly-expressed pro-totalitarian and anti-democratic features. Although it is flying in the face of fashion for anti-economism, the economic factor is exerting a considerable influence on value structures: the lower the level of material well-being, the higher the demands for a 'firm hand'; and vice versa: the better things get, the higher the value of freedom.

Young people are alarmed about their future, they fear the spectre of poverty, unemployment and loneliness; they are afraid of being deprived of the still remaining minimum of guarantees which they currently possess.

In the immediate future we may expect a sharp increase in com-mercialisation and rationalisation of everyday consciousness, first and foremost with young people. The increasing humanitarian development of education is intended to act as a counterbalance to this tendency and to avert any deformation of a young person's spiritual world.

Notes

See references to Ilynsky, Chapter 1.

8 The value orientations of Belorus youth

LARISSA TITARENKO

Introduction

According to globalization trends, one may observe certain common features of young people in all industrial countries, including those of the former USSR, such as Belorus, which are in the process of constructuring market relations and democratic political systems. These features are stimulating the integration of our countries into modern civilisation. Yet there are other characteristics of young people which reflect specific historical and social conditions in their development. Both trends are reflected in youth value-orientations.

Youth values in Belorus

Much of sociological research in Belorus, as in the former USSR as a whole, was focused on the problems of formation of youth value-orientations and on the role of various social institutions (family, school, mass media) in this process.[1]

In this paper, we refer to the results of sociological research on youth in Belorus, mainly conducted by staff in the Department of Sociology, Belarus State University. This empirical work enables us to analyse the problems and ask whether youth value orientations in Belorus are relevant to the level of industrial consciousness prevalent in the West.

First of all, we must establish whether Belorus youth identifies itself with the global community. According to our research in Minsk in 1993, an absolute majority of respondents identified themselves either with their 'small Motherland' (native town, village and so on) or with the country in which they live - i.e. the Belorus Republic. Only about 10 per cent identify themselves with Europe or with the global community. Such results are typical of Belorus, Lithuania, Kazakhstan and other young independent republics of the former USSR. They reflect the growth of a sense of political independence, on the one hand, and the low level of global consciousness, on the other.

Our research also shows that Belorus youth has no nationalistic orientations: for the absolute majority of young people, territorial (regional) affiliation is equal to their national affiliation. Such results are typical of modern industrial countries with a multi-ethnic population. This situation is the same for young people in Belorus as well as in the West.

We conclude that there are few orientations concerning regional and global characteristics that separate Western and Commonwealth of Independent States (CIS) youth. So it is more important for us to research the specific value-orientations of our young people and their origins. Let us consider the youth value system in Belorus under conditions of transition.

Youth values in the process of transition

In today's conditions of social instability and deepening socio-economic crisis, the problem of seeking an appropriate position in the social structure and the formation of life ideals are becoming increasingly difficult for youth. The tasks of the transition to market relations demand the creation of a real potential labour market and training labour power for these changes. This means we need to develop specific personal qualities, like personal responsibility, readiness to take risks, to adjust to the new economic situation, to do hard work for one's well-being in the future. Now these new qualities and labour-orientations are necessary not only for managers, businessmen, leaders of the private sector, but for all members of the system of market relations. In order to make the socio-economic reforms successful society needs simultaneous changes in the thinking of the majority of the population (at least the able-bodied population). Society has to create a popular readiness to live and work in a market economy. When such socio-psychological readiness is created, society will take a significant step forward.

Meanwhile, we are rejecting all the previous high-rank values for young people connected with the Soviet period (so called 'socialist values'): harmoniously developed personality, priority of common interests, collectivism, self-realisation of a person in work and so on. Today's young people cannot use the previous system of values as an orientation in situations of life choices, in the decision-making process. The crisis of erstwhile value-orientations is vividly manifest in the sphere of work (in relation to one's work and profession).

Value orientations in the sphere of work

As most sociological research in the former USSR shows[2] young respondents included labour and interesting work in the list of their life ambitions, which were absolute essential to be content. This means that when young people were asked 'What do you need most of all to be happy?', they answered 'an interesting job', 'a job I like', etc. Our research demonstrates that 'an interesting job' was one of the priorities of students - i.e. people who want to become specialists, professionals. More than 90 per cent of respondents in Minsk evaluate their opportunities of having a higher education as 'strong' and 'good'; 68 per cent answered that they had strong opportunities for improving their qualifications and 53 per cent for getting a job in their own specialism.[3] The life expectations of the majority of young people were connected with receiving education and a good job. They were optimistic about the future.

On the whole, all groups in the population, including youth, put top of their value hierarchy obtaining an interesting job. One can say that it became a tradition to consider work as an absolute unconditional value for socialist society and for every individual in it. This approach was closely connected with the Marxist theory of personal self-realisation through work. According to this theory, under socialist conditions labour is transformed into a vital need, a source of satisfaction and happiness. In reality, this was not so.

That is why, during the period of stagnation, alienation from work became more intensive, opportunities for self-realisation through work were limited and the social significance of highly qualified labour gradually fell.

As a result, a process of instrumentalization of work was underway in the 1980s. Work stopped being evaluated only according to content and people began to consider it as a source of well-being, a material means of existence. In our youth studies in Minsk in the mid-1980s,[4] about two-thirds of respondents said that they preferred socially-useful and interesting work, but the amount of money they received for this work was meaningful too. Among people aged 16-20, the social value of work was considered to be more important; among people from 21-30, the wages were considered to be a much more meaningful factor. To the question 'What is the essence of human life?', only one out of three respondents answered 'fruitful work for the benefit of society'.

At the same time, one in four respondents saw the essence of life in material well-being ('to have everything I need'). Our conclusion is that a shift from spiritual, traditionally widespread values to material values (money, consumer goods, well-being) began more than 20 years ago and embraced all groups in the population. The most evident manifestation of this shift took place in youth value orientations. This process was highly contradictory. When we consider the level of verbal, abstract opinions, creative work was rated quite high. But the ranking of high payment for work (whether skilled or not) rose from year to year in the hierarchy of values. For instance, our research in Minsk revealed that creative, interesting work took first or second position, while a highly paid job was ranked fifth or sixth. However, the ranking of interesting, not highly paid work was practically the same (from third to fifth position or about 30 per cent of respondents).[5]

Current trends

This situation has changed greatly over the last few years owing to the socio-economic crisis and high inflation of the early-mid 1990s. In 1993, only 37 per cent of Minsk respondents (among students) put interesting work on the list of major life values. This factor retained its third ranking, but some other factors occupied the same position. For example, violence was considered to be very important. This fact is new for our young people because in previous years only some schoolboys rated violence and brute strength highly (in comparison with other spiritual values).

We proposed a group of values closely connected with work (interesting profession, intellect, education, creativity). From 1987 to 1993, the average evaluation of the significance of these values more than halved. First of all, this concerns the values of study and education (where the reduction was from 39 per cent to 9 per cent). This figure reflects the disappointment of young people in education as a means to achieve life success and well-being. Young people rejected education even as a means of gaining higher wages and a professional career. Study and education are no longer considered to be either the end or the means for achieving other, more significant aims. One of the characteristics of the present situation is a transition to self-value of any human activity, which can provide a high quality of life. This is of great importance to those young people who represent the potential labour market (i.e. those who study). As for those young people who already work, the very state of employment became of great value to them (the content of work), because of the threat of unemployment. Of course, this situation does not stimulate initiative and creativity in their work.

This shift in the system of values is concerned with the new trend towards a decrease in skill, the skill culture of working people, towards a conformism in respect of unfavourable conditions of work, lack of social protection. With forthcoming unemployment, the most accessible and preferable professions for young people are becoming those that need rough manual labour and 'initiative' (racketeering, extortion) or the opportunity to receive a lot of money through illegal means (trade speculation, 'pseudotourism to Poland, Turkey, etc.). Only a small number of these young people have a real chance to become employers or manufacturers. As for the others, they have lost the old stimulus to work, but have not found a new one.

The situation among young graduates is different to some extent. Sociological research in Minsk in 1993 shows that about 50 per cent want to work in jobs relating to their degree, the rest are ready to change their profession or do not know what they want. About 55 per cent of respondents want to work in the private sector, in joint enterprises or co-operatives; only 27 per cent want to work in the state sector. The main demand for future work is a high salary (85 per cent) and the opportunity to receive a state apartment (45 per cent). Only one out of three respondents connects future work with the opportunity of enhancing professional culture, but one in four dreams of business trips abroad. Our modern young specialists are realistic in their estimate of the future: only 7 per cent are sure that everything will be fine with their job, and 50 per cent of respondents see real problems and contradictions in the process of getting a job. They believe only in their own abilities (40 per cent) or in relatives' help in finding work (35 per cent), in their friends (20 per cent), but not in the state labour service or local authorities (only 5-6 per cent of respondents).[6] These figures show the realism of our young specialists, on the one hand, and the lack of faith in government, state, social justice, on the other.

All these changes in work value orientations show the need to develop a new mechanism of motivation which would stimulate creative activity and youth initiative as well as new forms of self-realisation in work. But this mechanism has not yet taken shape. Many young people cannot find the necessary stimulus to work hard, apart from money.

High wages is naturally a strong stimulus. Unfortunately, it is not closely associated with the quality and quantity of work. So it often serves as an anti-stimulus and does not contribute to the growth of effectiveness of the current socio-economic reforms. Moreover, when payment becomes the main stimulus to work, it indicates the poor moral health of society and a decrease in the role of work as a basis for prosperity for the majority of the population.

Now many young people prefer pragmatic, utilitarian orientations in work. The above mentioned sociological research can be interpreted as a new labour paradigm (ideas about how to be a success). Skill as the means of life-success is replaced by pragmatism. In other words, such professional values as competance, initiative, expertise, education are less significant in youth consciousness than the capacity to make money (the latter belongs to the group material values whose importance is constantly growing).

Other youth value-orientations

Traditionally value-orientations on friendship, love and mutual respect in interrelationships were rated very highly among young people. Suffice it to say that they took second or third ranking in the hierarchy of values.[7] They reflected the orientation of society in the past on spiritual values. As far as young people were concerned, such a hierarchy reflected overall romanticism and a high level of trust among members of our society (i.e. preference for a collectivist way of life).

Nowadays the situation is as follows: this group of values (friendship, love, good understanding among people in a group) is still at the top of the hierarchy and more preferable than professional values (the difference between the two groups is twice as much in favour of inter-personal relationships). There are two modes of life: labour-oriented (work is the main social relationship) and family-oriented (family is the basis of a person's private life). But the overall evaluation of 'friendship values' has declined: for example, the category 'to have faithful friends' dropped from 91 per cent to 78 per cent and 'love' from 68 per cent to 48 per cent. At the same time, the second ranking in the overall hierarchy belongs to material values, such as 'money'. The significance of the group of material values has more than doubled. Now the ranking of material values is very close to that of inter-personal values.[8]

There are some contradictory trends in the process of changing youth values. One section of young people is seeking a firm grounding for their existence in private life and individual values (living for oneself and one's family, strengthening the family, believing in help from one's relatives). They reject values associated with socially useful labour, political activity, living for the collective, etc. They preserve some moral values concerning individual-family life, but they suffer from the loss of a mutual social system of values. The other section of young people has lost the moral and social background of life and does not believe in anything. They seek comfort, prosperity, enjoyment and prefer sex instead of family, power instead of friendship or an intellectual challenge, money instead of work. In conditions of a socio-economic crisis and moral vacuum, this section of youth can be considered as the lost generation, unable to contribute to the revival of our country.

Conclusion

We can conclude, therefore, that changes in youth value-orientations reflect the main trends in socio-economic development in Belorus. They have much in common with the changes in the value system in Russia, the Ukraine and other former Soviet Republics. Our main problem is to create new stable orientations in work, to overcome the moral vacuum, to give the younger generation a firm foundation for seeking a new status in the transition to a market economy.

Notes

1   See for example, *Urgent Problems of the Moral Upbringing of Students* (Minsk, 1985); *Moral Images of Soviet Youth* (Minsk, 1985) and L. Titarenko, *The Political Culture of Young People* (Minsk, 1989).

2   Ibid. See also G. Cherednichenko and B. Shubkin, *Youth is Coming* (Moscow, 1985); S. Ikonnikova, *Youth* (Leningrad, 1974) and A. Kozlov and V. Lisovsky, *Young People: Formation of Modes of Life* (Moscow, 1986).

3   See Titarenko, 1989 op cit.

4   Ibid.

5   Ibid.

6   *Social and Managerial Aspects of Economic Restructuring Survey* (Minsk, 1993).

7   V. Sokolov, *Sociology of Moral Development of the Individual* (Moscow, 1986).

8   *Social and Managerial*, 1993 op cit.

PART III

EASTERN EUROPE

9 Young people between war and peace in the former Yugoslavia

Introduction

War was raging and famine and disease plagued the land; the shortage of food was so severe that even human flesh was eaten. Crowds of people roamed the country crying 'Peace, Peace!'.

This is not - or not yet - a report from the war stricken areas of former Yugoslavia, but a description of European conditions in the middle of the eleventh century, recorded in Radolphus Glaber's *Chronicle*. This description of human suffering during wartime contains an obvious basic paradox: namely, for the starving and bewildered people, the main need was for peace and not bread, as might be expected. At the same time, it implies that some others, or even those same people, once regarded war as a great objective. Perhaps that is why years of peace were so scarce in human history, so out of proportion to the years when war was raging somewhere else in the world. And each war tragedy opens the question of peace as a value and of war as a responsibility. How do young people in the republics of the former Yugoslavia respond to this? And why should their answers bear any particular relevance? Simply because they are the main fodder and the victims of 'the masters of war', the 'cannon fodder' fed to the 'gods of war'. Besides, the outcome of the Yugoslav war drama and the future of nations to which these young people belong largely depend on their attitudes.

Past legacies

Yugoslavia was twice made by war and twice destroyed by it. It was founded on a 'powder keg' - a popular metaphor for the Balkan Peninsula coined by political strategists - in the aftermath, and as a result, of the First World War. Its territory was the border-area of two great Empires destroyed in the war, the Hapsburg Monarchy and the Ottoman Empire. The creation of the new state was due not only to the combined skills of the Great Powers which, led by Wilson's doctrine (that is, by a system of peace contracts), shaped post-war European order (which did not last for more than two decades). The state of the Southern Slav nations was also a long-expected fulfilment of their needs and interests, an answer to their age-old striving to free themselves from the domination of imperial forces. Its creation was preceded by struggles for freedom, integrity, equality and autonomy which lasted more than a century and which took place in a geographical region that had been divided, mainly by force, through the centuries. It was a kind of border area of great empires and civilisations. For centuries, Austria and Turkey were using the mechanisms of great rival powers to rule part of what had now become an independent state of Southern Slavs, and thus produced a kind of border and intolerant mentality, characterised by a collective sense of life and suspicion towards every alien and strongly individual element that, as such, does not fit into the traditional frame of the community.

One of the authorities on the Balkan Peninsula, the anthropologist Jovan Cvijic, described five cultural zones which constituted the new state community: the patriarchal, Byzanto-Tzintzarian, Italian, Central European and Turkish. The 249,000 square kilometres of the underdeveloped and unintegrated country were populated by 12 million people belonging to a variety of ethnically kindred and mutually hostile nations. Over the centuries they were serving different masters and in the First World War they were fighting one another. During the war (in which Serbia, for instance, lost more than a third of its population) even the members of one and the same nation were fighting against each other. The religious divisions were no less acute. A spirit of intolerance prevailed among members of the Catholic, Orthodox and Muslim religious communities. The members of ethnically close nations were believers in religions that carried on the age-old quarrels.

As to the possibility of economic integration on the territory of the newly-founded state, the situation was no better. Dominant economic forces differed from one province to another: some still had a patriarchal and tribal economy; in others small agricultural properties prevailed, while others were gradually pervaded by the European ways of industrialisation.

The basis for a possible social integration and industrial modernisation in the newly-established country was all too weak and heterogeneous. However, the inter-war period was marked by attempts to constitute an integrated civil society and reconcile the essential economic, political and cultural differences by means of authoritarian policies.

The Second World War not only destroyed the first, civil Yugoslav state, but at the same time created a new 'socialist' Yugoslavia. Thus the continuity of the civil social development was severely interrupted and once more Yugoslavia had to start afresh as an underdeveloped, unintegrated and incomplete civil society. In these circumstances, the 'socialist' attempt was almost bound to be authoritarian and even more totalitarian in nature. In the final analysis, the system of 'self-management socialism' or 'socialism with a human face' appeared to be much closer to the systems of 'real socialism' in the East European countries than to the principles of human freedom and justice. Therefore, its breakdown should be seen in terms of the historic collapse of the 'global socialist system', which is best symbolised by the fall of the Berlin Wall.

The younger generation and the civil war

Today former Yugoslavia's younger generation has to face a Civil War and a social tragedy which often becomes a personal trauma. How do they respond to this extremely difficult situation? The answer to this question still lies in the sphere of surmise; there are no reliable data, nor serious research. Generally speaking, the response of the younger generation is ambiguous: a part of it was involved in the war machinery, while the other part avoided fighting in the war which was regarded as 'somebody else's war', sometimes at a very high price.

In late 1991, a survey was conducted among Belgrade students; it showed that 54 per cent of the respondents were against the war with Croatia, while 37 per cent wanted its continuation - on the basis that the threatened Serbs in Croatia needed brotherly help. The same research showed that 77 per cent of respondents agreed with the statement that no war aims were worth so many human casualties and so much destruction, while 78 per cent concurred with the claim that the authorities of the confronted sides were using the war as a means of achieving their specific political objectives. Other research only further asserted this ambiguity of attitudes. For instance, when participants in the student protest in June 1991 were asked 'how would you behave in the event of a foreign military intervention on Serbia's territory?', the answers were divided into two equal groups: 54 per cent claimed that they would join those who defended the country, while 46 per cent stated that they would try to find a sure refuge.

Innocent victims or willing participants?

In the civil and religious war on the territory of the former Yugoslavia, there are so many innocent victims and war crimes, so much profiteering and banditry, that no participant in the war could be considered innocent. Still, the unfortunate young people involved in the war should not be treated as 'dogs of war' without reservation. Should those 50 young men, recruits of the regular Yugoslav army, who were sent to Slovenia almost unarmed and were killed be considered war criminals? Of course, the policy which imposed those sufferings on them *was* criminal. But those who were regularly recruited had few opportunities to evade war service. The recruiting was carried out by all confronted sides; and not only young men, but middle aged too were enlisted. In this war a significant number of older people voluntarily risked their lives to protect the younger soldiers.

What possibilities had a young Serb from Gospic, or a Croat of the same age from Convale near Dubrovnik, or a Muslim from Mostar, to escape death on their doorstep or in a concentration camp? To those people whose very existence was threatened nobody could deny the right to defend it. They cannot be easily condemned for taking part in the war (which by no means implies their right to do atrocities to the other side).

Volunteers

The third largest group of young participants in the war consists of volunteers - Slovene, Croat, Serb and Muslim. Many of them never lived in the areas in which they fought, nor even in Yugoslavia. Most were either victims or protagonists of war propaganda. Motivated by national hatred, revenge and robbery, they added a new ferocity to the war. Still, even some among them died in the belief that they were defending 'holy' national interests. An analyst eager to encompass all the varieties of this group will need extremely sensitive tools.

A dirty war

Finally, this war is made up of small, personal, dirty wars. The confronted ethnic groups have been using criminals and delinquents for the dirtiest aspects of the war. War propaganda has often celebrated those young criminals as war and national heroes; some of them even became members of parliament or media celebrities. They were licensed to carry out crimes and robberies, but after playing at the role were pulled off the stage or even killed.

Protests against the war

The 'anti-war' side of the youth population is no less diversified: from those who are just frightened by the war to the active peacemakers engaged in the peace movement. We should not forget the deserters, who found themselves in a difficult situation. Nobody knows the exact number of them in Croatia, Serbia and Bosnia and Herzegovina. The official data were never published, but it is clear that the percentage of Army deserters differs from one place to another, and from one region to another. Their number is insignificant even among Serbs, whose attitudes towards the army are traditionally positive; and we need not mention that in the regions of Serbia populated mainly or entirely by Albanians, the number of recruits is negligible.

The odyssey of the young deserters from the army does not end by the semi-legal crossing of the state border, but begins with it. European governments treat these young men as trespassers and require them to prove their desertion by an official *written document* or *a court martial sentence*, which is fragrant nonsense. Official Europe issues numerous resolutions, declarations and severe warnings to urge a peaceful solution to the Balkan crisis, and at the same time pushes these young men back into the maelstrom of war. Moreover, in all the Yugoslav republics, young deserts are looked upon as traitors to the national cause and threatened by court trials.

Refugees

The second, much larger group of young people who fled the war, consists of refugees, now living in the newly-established states on the territory of former Yugoslavia, as well as in other European and non-European countries. Significant and reliable data about them are very scarce. For instance, we know that 42.6 per cent of refugees in Serbia (or 226,000 out of a total of 530,000) are children and young people under 18 years of age. Their position is hardly satisfactory. In addition to the usual difficulties of procuring shelter, regular schooling and even food, young men over 18 who find refuge in the former Yugoslavia are faced with the very real danger of being recruited by force and sent to the front.

Victims of war and ethnic cleansing

The third group, whose position is probably the most tragic of all, consists of young victims of war and ethnic cleansing, who are maimed or wounded or banished from home. Those are Serbs, Croats and Muslims. At this moment, the Muslims from various parts of Croatia and Bosnia and Herzegovina are probably the most numerous among them. Their homes and schools have been burned, their families destroyed or dispersed throughout the world. Nobody knows the exact number of these hopeless 'Palestinians' of today's Europe.

The brain drain

All the republics of former Yugoslavia, recently established as states, are facing the severe problem of a brain drain, or the emigration of their young intellectuals. There have been many guesses at the number of those who left with university degrees: for example, the Belgrade press has estimated that 200,000 young people emigrated from Serbia alone. What we know for certain is that in 1992 a 1,000 members of Belgrade University staff left Serbia, some of them for good. They succeeded in finding more or less adequate jobs in academic institutions of highly developed countries. Even more reliable is the fact that from Belgrade's Institute for Electronics, 240 researchers emigrated in 1992, and in the first six months of 1993, 180 of their colleagues followed suit. These were mostly young researchers. The situation in other cultural centres of former Yugoslavia is approximately the same.

Conclusions

On the territory of former Yugoslavia, young people are getting killed or exiled. We should not forget that they are potential fathers and mothers. Thus the dwarf states, proud successors of the former Yugoslavia, are being transformed into societies without any cultural or other perspective. They are being left without any biological substratum or brains. The important question is whether the energy and enthusiasm of a very thin stratum of student youth will be sufficient for any substantial turnaround in the situation. The messages of Belgrade students were: 'We don't want war', 'The country is fed up with bloodshed - it needs living people', 'Students want peace, democracy and freedom for everybody', 'We don't want to exchange our university books for guns', and so forth. The question to ask is what will happen first: the breakdown of society or the triumph of these noble youth aspirations?

If the creation of the two (authoritarian) Yugoslavias required two world wars, and if their destruction required one world and one extremely brutal civil war, one can only dread the possibility of creating a third Yugoslavia. Or perhaps the fatal disease of the first and second Yugoslavia, namely the extinguishing of a democratic alternative, can be cured? This multi-cultural, multi-ethnic and multi-religious region deserves a better fate. If we manage to survive and preserve our human sub-stratum, one day the differences may become our dearest treasure and peace our supreme value. The essential condition of such a possibility is to open our hearts to the spirit of tolerance.

10 Xenophobia and ethnocentricity in the former German Democratic Republic

JACQUELINE HENNIG

Introduction

We are confronted today in Europe with mounting tendencies of ethnocentrism, even xenophobia. The increase in nationalism, along with antagonism to foreigners, is not only observable as new ethnic groups enter the political arena, but also in modern nation states which were supposed to be multicultural societies. Ethnic distinctiveness is becoming a substantial element of youth culture, at least with regard to some young people. We find several approaches and attempts to interpret these attitudes and practices. My own research is based on recent empirical work in East Germany.

The more individuals and groups are anxious about their social identity, the more they develop demarcation lines against strangers. In troubled times, when identities are threatened by social insecurity, ethnocentricity serves as a major frame of reference, while foreigners gain less acceptance than under former stable economic and political conditions. In particular, those age cohorts of the younger generation who are in the critical phase of searching for a proper identity are significantly involved with protecting their own ethnicity against influences from outside which they regard as 'alien' and 'somewhat dangerous'. In the extreme case, some groups, almost without exception male, tend to exaggerate their mistrust and prejudices in open hostility and xenophobia.

Some empirical findings

In April and May 1993, a team of the Berlin Institute of Applied Youth Research carried out a study among teenagers in three small towns near Berlin. The random sample consisted of 619 school students in the age-range 12-16 years. An equal distribution among age cohorts and gender was ensured. The method we used for our investigation was the questionnaire.

Out of dozens of figures and tables contained in our Research Report, I shall select only four which refer mostly to my theme.

The responses to the crucial item in our questionnaire (too many foreigners in Germany) seem high. Table 10.1 below shows that more than half the respondents (56.7 per cent) fear that too many foreigners have invaded the nation's territory, whereas only about a quarter feels that although many non-Germans are living here they can still be tolerated.

Table 10.1
Assessments of the desirability of foreigners
in Germany (in %)

Viewpoint	Percentage
Much too much	12.1
Too much	44.6
High, but tolerable	26.3
Undecided	16.9

When asked whether they could live with foreign newcomers in a close neighbourhood, where immigrants are usually collected at refugee homes waiting for a permanent visa, the response frequencies point in the same direction:

Table 10.2
Attitudes towards living in close proximity
with foreigners in former DDR (in %)

Response	*Per cent*
Fully agree	15.3
More agree than disagree	19.3
More disagree than agree	33.2
Completely disagree	31.6

Again the resistance to foreigners is much greater than acceptance. To have new immigrants living in the home country, even in the home town of our respondents, evokes a negative response from almost two-thirds.

On the other hand, there is a strong belief in the importance of being a member of the German nation. Nearly 60 per cent of the young people regard German nationality of great value for their self-esteem and status, avoiding the inferiority typical of non-Germans.

Table 10.3
The relevance of being German in former DDR (in %)

Response	*Per cent*
Very important	42.3
Quite important	16.9
Less important	25.5
Not important	14.8

The importance of age and gender

What is interesting is the variation of attitudes according to age and gender. Our findings clearly indicate a higher percentage rejecting foreigners in the older cohort (14-16 years). For instance, 78.5 per cent of respondents aged 16 are hostile to 'too many foreigners' in the country, whereas only 34.6 per cent of the 12 year olds are similarly troubled. To live with new immigrants close to their homes is unacceptable to 84.6 per cent of the 16 year olds while the percentage decreases by half for the 12 year olds, of which only 40.3 per cent show opposition.

Evidently the age cohort confronted with the difficulties of transferring from school to work, with the risks surrounding it, constructs social reality in quite a different way than do younger pupils. Therefore, they form an image of foreigners as being potential rivals or as persons creating unpredictable and uncontrollable situations. The ascribed attributes are sometimes nothing less than stigmatisation.

Male respondents are significantly more intolerant than their female counterparts. For instance, 65.3 per cent of males compared with 47.8 per cent of female students fear that too many foreigners have embarked upon the 'German boat'. Deep mistrust, complete disagreement about living in close proximity to an immigrant exist among 62.2 per cent of males in comparison with 37.8 per cent of the females in the population interviewed.

At first glance, that fact is surprising, because one could have expected young women to feel more disturbed by the presence of strangers whose behaviour is somewhat unpredictable. However, we may explain the female tolerance by socialisation concepts. Female socialisation aims at, or often results in, the capacity of compliance, balancing discordances and mollifying tensions. By contrast, boys are usually socialised towards domination, taking a firm stand in confrontation and not giving in.

Table 10.4 below shows that male youngsters are also much more ready to take violent action against immigrants, although - in general - open militancy by young people exists only in a small proportion of the sample. A willingness to use violent action is significantly more typical for boys (19.5 per cent) as against girls (4.9 per cent). This means that every fifth person among the males is committed to aggression against immigrants. However, in general, the activist kernel in favour of violent action only constitutes a tenth of the teenagers of our sample. That proportion correspondents with several other findings.

Table 10.4

Attitudes regarding violence against foreigners

in former DDR (in %)

Response	*Per cent*
In favour of violence	12.2
No brutality, but Germans are always right	9.5
Disregard injuries	7.1
Neutrality because of lack of support	13.3
Activity in order to mobilise support	19.1
Uncertainty about intervention	38.9

The four tables show that ethnocentrism is widespread, while xenophobia among young Germans is significant in minor groups. Therefore, discrimination practices, accentuating boundaries between Germans and non-Germans, are characteristic of a major part of the younger generation which seems to need ethnic, national distinctiveness and needs to belong in order to anchor its identity. Ethnocentricity of that kind involves an incapacity to acknowledge cultural differences and prejudices regarding foreigners as inferior. The latest reluctance to accept or even hostility against immigrants among a considerable part of the population could be regarded as support for the manifest xenophobia and violent capacity of extremists.

Conclusions

Extremism in the form of xenophobia cannot be overcome by idealist concepts of education. It is so much rooted in the broader social context that the appeal for mutual understanding appears to be too weak to change rigid attitudes and irrational behavioural patterns like those involving aggression against foreigners. Therefore, it is absolutely necessary for the state authorities to counteract violent tendencies. However, even state power has only a small chance of tackling the phenomenon if there is public support for and confidence in state actions, and if, furthermore, the law is executed firmly and strictly against discriminating practices. At the moment, sadly, both preconditions are absent. Public support is more in favour of restrictive measures against immigration; and legislation is more in favour of ethnocentrism than of equal rights for foreigners.

Nevertheless, multicultural education programmes can reach the majority, which is either neutral or searching for national identity. Whether education is powerful enough to overcome strong prejudices and widespread segregation remains to be seen. There is a long way to go until this desirable state of affairs will occur.

11 Youth and society in Slovakia

LADISLAV MACHACEK

Sociography of the youth movement in Slovakia

The democratic changes in the political system of Czechoslovakia are closely connected with the revolutionary action of the younger generation, especially students. The moral and social results of its natural orientation on the future has acted as a detonator for releasing a mass civic movement of dissatisfaction which swept away the old structures. The real destruction of the political system of the 'party-state' began when an independent student movement, represented first of all by the Students Union of Slovakia and the Slovak Unity of Secondary School Students, was formed and it separated from one of the most important elements of the system - the uniform youth organisation (Socialist Union of Youth).

Changes in the youth associations as an important component of civic society were achieved at the meeting of two parallel developments. In a relatively short time the Socialist Union of Youth split into several independent children's and youth organisations (Pioneers, the Tree of Life, Association of Slovak Students, Union of Youth). Their programmes were reoriented and reformed. Simultaneously, new children's and youth organisations and movements based on specific interests and ideological principles were created. Youth organisations and movements closely connected with the parties they belong to have the most influence. A motley mosaic of youth movements and organisations, clubs, unions etc. is the result of these processes.

In harmony with pluralism as a political notion, making possible multiplicity and variety in political life and a coalition for solving social problems, we can identify different categories in the youth movement in Slovakia:

1   Organisations representing single social groups of youth (Slovak Association of Slovak Students, Slovak Union of Secondary-School Students, Association of Working Youth, Union of Youth).

2   Organisations grouping youth on ethnic principles (Union of Hungarian Student Youth, Hungarian Union of Youth, Union of Hungarian Scouts).

3   Professional associations of youth (Association of Students of Business and Management, Forum of Youth Theatre Actors in Slovakia, Association of Architecture Students, Akademos-Society of Friends of Education and Science, Unity of Youth Contractors).

4   Unions based on special interests and associations of youth (Union of Associations based on special interest, Youth Scientific-Technical Association for Youth, Sciences and Technology, Movement of the Tree of Life, Association of Clubs of the Tree of Life, Associations of Youth-Depeche Mode Fans of Slovakia, Folklore Union of Slovakia, Club for Non-traditional Sports, Stefanik, Students Associations).

5   Organisations and associations for children and for work with children (Junak, Pioneer, Children's Fund, Movement of Christian Families).

6   Children's and youth organisations of a political character or close to the political parties or movements (Young Liberals, Democratic Youth of Slovakia, Christian-Democratic Youth of Slovakia, Clubs of Young Communists, Union of Slovak Youth, Social-Democratic Youth of Slovakia); and finally,

7   Associations of youth organisations (Law Protected Property Union of Children and Youth Organisations of Slovakia, Slovak Youth Council).

At present the complete redistribution of the original united youth organisation (Socialist Union of Youth) has not been achieved. Neither has the process of pluralisation of the youth movement been culminated. The real character or profile of the subjects of the youth movement cannot be fully manifested. A part will not change to real youth movements, but to enterprises offering expert services to youth and their organisations. They are associations which arose in the revolutionary movement, but only their regulations and programmes remain as a subject for sociological and historical research.

Influence of the State on youth

Rising unemployment among young people was a surprise for everyone, but most of all for the students of secondary schools and universities who (sometimes against the will of their teachers and parents) had started the revolution, participating in demonstrations at Prague and Bratislava main squares which brought an end to the communist regime.

The euphoria from dismantling the totalitarian dictatorship of the Communist Party and its administrative-bureaucratic state machine is being overshadowed by complex feelings of coming to terms with the consequences of economic reform.

The paternalism of the totalitarian regime created within society a specific value system, in which the decisive position was devoted to social security, represented by the right to free education, to free choice of profession and the right to work. Sociological surveys confirmed that young people were giving credit to these values. Slovak youth, however, connected such values as 'the development of science and technology' and the implementation of people's ideas and notions with the advantages of capitalist society. Young people did not conceive that these social advantages had to be paid for by limitation of the exercise of their performance orientation and personal responsibility. Such a social schizophrenia of the past assumes new forms. The first consequences of the economic reform are beginning to manifest themselves in the labour market.

The Czecho-Slovak Federal Government emphasised in its programme that social security could not be closely connected with the all-embracing care of the state, but rather with the maximum efforts of each individual member of the younger generation. The programme of economic reform offered them opportunities - but opportunities with responsibility.

The risk of unemployment to young people was admitted at the turn of 1989/1990 primarily in connection with the principles of liberalisation of students, admission of students to secondary schools and universities. Some of these schools and universities always enjoyed great interest on the part of young people. The survey among 1,055 women in this period confirmed that some 30 per cent realised the risk of unemployment. They gave preference particularly to the possibility that liberalisation would help in revealing new talents (24.5 per cent), it would stimulate increased efforts on the part of students (18.9 per cent) and reduce the scope for favouritism and bribery in admission of students (17.3 per cent). The survey showed that young people should have a guaranteed right to work in the area in which they studied or were trained (58.3 per cent) or outside the original area (29 per cent) for at least 1-3 years. Only 8.5 per cent of surveyed women believed that 'there is no need to lay down the right to work for youth specifically'. As the Government put it in its original programme: 'The social content of the economic programme tries to gain maximal fairness for everybody'.

Youth unemployment

In the meantime, the situation changed substantially. Unemployment became a reality. The unemployment of young people who had completed basic and secondary schools, as well as universities, is now beginning to be seen as a destructive force threatening the organisation and cohesion of society.

On 31 March 1991 as many as 184,612 unemployed were registered. The proportion of unemployment is 2.55 per cent - 3.83 per cent in the Slovak Republic and 1.94 per cent in the Czech Republic. The worst situation among the particular districts is in the Czech Republic in Znojmo district (4 per cent) and, in the Slovak Republic, in Rimavska Sobota district (7.25 per cent).

Several general trends can be seen: women suffer from unemployment more than men; less able-bodied citizens more than healthy citizens, Gypsies (Rom) more than others; the younger age groups more than the older ones. For instance, the proportion of citizens in the workforce under 30 years is 26 per cent, but their proportion among the unemployed is 48 per cent.

Particularly alarming is the trend of growing unemployment among school leavers. Of the total number of basic school pupils, who were to enter the labour market in 1990 (9,016), 51.9 per cent were not employed by 30 April 1991. Of the total number of secondary school students 10,013 were not employed, representing a total of 5.5 per cent. And, last but not least, of 20,392 university graduates, 1,887 were not employed, which represents 9.25 per cent.

Graduates from secondary schools and universities have appeared repeatedly among applicants for employment via employment offices, especially in Slovakia. This phenomenon is connected with demographic trends in the 1970s and with an accelerated decrease of vacancies for workers.

The social youth net

In its resolution No. 275/90 the Government of the Slovak Republic adopted the proposal of the Ministry of Education to organise half-year specialisation studies for unemployed school-leavers aimed at their improvement in languages, programming, management skills. They are entitled to obtain grants amounting to 1,400 crowns monthly. Thirty six per cent of unemployed school-leavers were involved; 619 out of 801 who started studies in September 1990 finished in March 1991.

From the labour market stand-point these measures were appraised as a temporary substitution for a social network. Reimbursement to employers of six months wages, or a portion thereof, on conclusion of a labour agreement for each school leaver represents an additional measure which has the same purpose.[1]

Some 3,800 school-leavers used this opportunity, together with economic stimulation measures for admission of school-leavers, representing more than 12 per cent from the total number in 1990. In 1991, the above-mentioned arrangements were applied again. We do not want to conceal the fact that the provision of financial security for school-leavers in the form of fixed monthly amounts brings about a demotivating effect.[2] An increased misuse of these benefits by the employer is expected. Despite all these facts, the two measures found a positive response because they represent an element within the organisation of general welfare labour activities, re-qualification, short-term stays abroad, promotion of young people who plan to set up small businesses.

The programmes of protection and promotion of young people elaborated by the youth departments at the Ministries of Education, Youth and Sport of the Czech Republic and Slovak Republic represent a specific proposition. These programmes were implemented in 1992. A Research Institute of Labour and Social Matters survey in Bratislava confirmed that 51.9 per cent of the enterprises and organisations consider that the tax and financial intervention of the state for admitting school-leavers is unavoidable.

Unemployment among young people is seen as a major factor disabling their participation in social life, participation understood in the sense of 'a share in decision making' and simultaneously 'assuming responsibility for themselves and their friends'. Unemployment of young people may instigate the development of a specific social network, which would not be completed without civic associations and movements promoting self-help and helping to eliminate social problems and obstacles to youth participation.

At present, the development of the youth service which would come from the hidden potential of the civic initiatives and movements and which would engage young people themselves in the solution to social problems is impossible without adequate state support during transition from state to private ownership. Such support is needed for the self-help movement of unemployed young people in the form of the 'Club of Young Unemployed' (or KMN). The initial idea of KMN has been put forward in Slovakia by one of the few youth movements which remained active among young workers after November 1989: the Association of Working Youth of Slovakia. This initiative gradually assumed new shape. The process may be characterised as a transition from charity to entrepreneurship. In the beginning, the Clubs of Young Unemployed were established spontaneously in 15 districts (50 per cent of districts in Slovakia) and their main objective was the creation of possibilities to meet each other, exchange information, tackle some problems involved in contracts with employment offices, self-help, a baby-sitter service during re-qualification courses for young unemployed people, psychological counselling, organisation of leisure-time activities etc. Only young people involved in re-organising, conversion of the arms-manufacturing industries, and closing down of workplaces were accepted as members. The efforts aimed at spreading the functions of KMN to other areas meant obtaining larger funds from various sources. For this reason, the 'Social fund for Young Unemployed in Slovakia' was established, collecting not only financial contributions but gifts as well. The funds for the activities of the Fund are supplied from short-term, social welfare activities of KMN members.

This form of economic activity gave rise to a business venture project 'Youth Labour Service' (or Students Labour Service) intended to create an opportunity for business activity of students or working youth, to allow the young unemployed to acquire additional sources of income in accordance with legal regulations, or extend their educational level and qualifications by experience, or to stimulate them to become involved in a re-qualification scheme.

Conclusions

It would probably be premature to try to evaluate the activities of the self-help movement pursued in the form of Clubs for the Young Unemployed. But this is a phenomenon which deserves the attention of the state authorities, local government and sociologists. Various measures adopted by the state quite often encounter a lack of understanding and even disbelief. The reason is that work with young people is quite often implemented in a paternalistic spirit: the state provides young people with support to survive and to pacify frustration. The principle of measures for young people being implemented primarily through young people themselves is being accepted only gradually. This principle, however, may be introduced only when the state can cure the illness of the totalitarian period; this illness is centralism, which manifests itself in the form of a lack of desire to strengthen the powers of cities and communities, or the powers of individual regions. The Charter on Participation of Young People in the Life of Communities and Regions, elaborated in the European Council, indicates how far our society is from pluralistic democracy in which civic society has a balanced background in the community and not only the state.

Notes

1   The proposal for a measure aimed at raising the financial interest of the employer in creating vacancies using a financial contribution not exceeding 1,200 crowns was prepared by the Ministry of Labour and Social Matters and the Ministry of Finance of the Czech Republic as well. However owing to the decreasing number of unemployed school-leavers at the end of 1990, this programme has not been launched.
2   The World Bank requires support of this kind to be bound only to those who had lost or left their previous professions, i.e. it should not cover school-leavers who have not succeeded in finding employment.

12 Youth beliefs and values in Bulgaria

LYDIA YORDANOVA

Introduction

Young people are the least satisfied section of the population in regard to Bulgaria's reforms. Only 5 per cent of young people aged 18-30 years interviewed in October 1993 were content with the direction and speed of the reforms. For every fourth young man nothing has changed. According to the opinion of half of them, the changes taking place are too slow and insufficient. More than half the young people believe that Bulgaria will remain a poor country in their lifetime.

Every second young person does not believe in any political power whatsoever and half of our respondents state that they will not vote; the rest do not consider anyone worth voting for. Now, over four years after the start of the changes, we are witnessing a peculiar lack of orientation and political apathy among young people. At present, the distrust of the young towards politics and politicians is the same as that of adults. This is a picture exactly opposite to that which we discovered in our research in 1989 and 1990.

Every fourth adult works overtime in order to receive additional income. Young people who earn additional money from overtime amount to 35 per cent. This and other data are presented in Tables 12.1-12.3.

Changes in values

Family and money are the two most important things in the lives of young people. This matches the value priorities of the population generally. Their importance increases as the value of work and leisure time decreases. The value of politics falls with 41 per cent of young people, compared to the autumn of 1990. Exactly the same is the growth in the share of extreme sceptics in regard to politics. Similar processes are evident among adults too, although they do not have such drastic quantitative measures.

Table 12.1
Prioritising value orientations, Bulgaria 1990-93

Please define the value in your life of the following:
(% of those interviewed)

	October 1990		*October 1992*		*September 1993*	
	a	*b*	*a*	*b*	*a*	*b*
Work	91	0	85	6	78	10
Family	96	0	96	1	94	1
Friends and contacts	77	2	83	4	67	6
Leisure	73	4	75	7	49	16
Politics	45	13	28	27	16	44
Religion	27	35	41	20	20	48
Business	-	-	30	40	22	50
Money	-	-	-	82	-	2
Sexual life	-	-	-	-	30	32

Notes: The difference up to 100 per cent is due to vague answers or 'NO ANSWER' responses.

a = very important
b = of no importance

Religion was important in the life of nearly half the young people in 1992, but it lost its position in the ranking-list of youth values in 1993 and remains important only for adults. Probably freedom to believe has been the real value, which now, after the flow of time, has lost its attractiveness.

Obviously, the religious groups which are very widespread in the country cannot rely on the values of religion. In spite of the fact that every fifth urban young person has come into contact with religious sects, the very strategy of those sects is mainly based on knowing the psychological and social problems of certain categories of young people. The data obtained show that the sects are most careful with active Orthodox religious young people.

On the whole, the changing values of young people are dominated by a return to the family and relatives, seen as the bastion of survival and prosperity. Close to the family is the basic pragmatic dominating value of the young - money. Work is no longer a sufficient or sufficiently reliable source of income or prosperity (in future as well as at present). Leisure time is generally becoming infused by the formula 'time is money' and spending it is accepted to be a luxury that spoils its new role in society. Friendship is also undergoing serious problems. More than two-thirds of people who declare they do not believe in anything, in fact show a decrease in the value of friendship in their life. Thus it appears to be only natural that young people are following a trend more characteristic of adults i.e. to enter into conflicts with friends and relatives on matters of politics, land and property, inheritance, etc. In that situation, young people more and more clearly understand that they are living in a society in which happiness is not simply measured by money, but it depends directly on the amount of money one has. For that reason, while in 1990 and 1991, youth criticism was directed towards the *nomenklatura*, it now points to the *nouveau riche* and speculators. 'Money', once considered a 'dirty' word, is replaced now by the 'dirty' word 'business'. One who is a businessman is rich, which means s/he is bad. This can be easily explained, bearing in mind that young people are the most marginal group in society since in present conditions they are forced to aspire to a certain standard and prosperity, like adults, who hanker after their irretrievably lost standards.

Table 12.2
Value orientations of Bulgarian youth 1990-93

Please define the value in your life of the following:
(% share of those young people interviewed aged 18-30)

	October 1990		October 1992		September 1993	
	a	*b*	*a*	*b*	*a*	*b*
Work	86	1	90	3	82	5
Family	93	1	94	2	94	1
Friends and contacts	87	1	94	0	81	2
Leisure	81	1	90	4	65	6
Politics	49	9	21	26	8	51
Religion	-	-	31	20	15	55
Business	-	-	47	19	35	33
Money	-	-	-	-	86	1
Sexual life	-	-	-	-	62	7

Note: The difference up to 100 per cent is due to vague answers or
'NO ANSWER' responses.

a = very important
b = of no importance

Young people clearly distinguish between a political and an economic elite,
although they are apt to define politicians as being wealthy. According to
National Public Opinion Centre (NAPOC) surveys, politics is 11 times less
important than money to young people. This is an indication that we are
now witnessing a generation that is first to slam the doors on political
emotions. At the same time, surveys showed that we are dealing with a life -
and generation - choice of values which does not influence the high (ever

growing) forbearance of youth towards people interested in politics or people of different opinions than theirs. The question of forbearance with adults is much more difficult, since they believe that harmony of political ideas is the basis and the major part of contracts in the family, professional or just everyday life. At present, politics concerns every third young person interviewed and this mainly in a pragmatic way. The problem is whether politicians will be able to secure preferences for the young. In this context, every third young person states that s/he is expecting financial support from the party s/he supports. A political career is not among the priorities of youth today. In such a situation, even contacts for exchanging political ideas shift to contacts and friendly relations based on common pragmatic interests.

What do Bulgarian young people believe in?

In a late 1993 NAPOC public opinion poll this question touched the most sensitive parts of mass consciousness as far as values are concerned.

A comparison between the beliefs of young people and adults shows that the most important difference is the stronger belief of the young in themselves and their relatives. At the same time, the young are more pragmatic in their beliefs; only a small number of them believe in general ideas and postulations, behind which past and present ideological schemes can be observed. A considerable part of young people relate this question to religion, hence their greater tendency (compared to adults) to declare a belief in God (Jesus Christ, Allah). Young people and adults are equally desperate and disillusioned. A high number of those interviewed of different ages answered ' I do not believe in anything'. This is the opinion of 21-23 per cent of respondents. An analysis - through a series of key questions - makes clear the reasons for the disillusionment of some young people, as well as the priority belief of others.

First, who are the young people that do not believe in anything? Most of them are relatively lukewarm towards politics as well as those who value friendship less and less. They are mainly poorly educated people and those with a low qualification, who do realise their poor opportunities to work in market conditions and achieve much. They live mostly in villages.

Second, who are the young people that believe in themselves alone and in their closest relatives? Most of them have been disaffected by politics. They consider their standard normal and they look upon poverty as something resulting from the market economy. They do not dramatise objective difficulties in life. They are highly educated and live in larger towns.

Table 12.3
Youth beliefs in Bulgaria, October 1993

What do you believe in?
(1,126 respondents)

	% of total interviewed	aged 18-30 % share
I do not believe in anything	23	22
God (Jesus Christ, Allah)	22	28
Myself and my family	20	31
Good, love and chance	8	5
The future	3	1
The Bulgarian socialist party	2	1
Common-sense	2	1
Fate/providence	2	1
Work	2	1
Truth/Justice	1	1
The Union of Democratic Forces	1	1
Business, initiative and money	1	1
No answer	14	16

Note: The question was asked in a very broad way. Some respondents (though a small number) marked more than one answer.

Third, who are the young people who believe in God (Jesus Christ, Allah)? Above all, the majority consider religion as a real value in their lives. They live in villages and small towns. Many belong to ethnic minorities. They are poorly educated, women are dominant. They are young people who stand aside from pragmatic values. This is only natural, bearing in mind that for them money is important only as a means of survival; so they make up for their falling living standards through religion. The group of those believing in God is close only to the group of the most elderly (above 60 years), which suggests a similar and low financial status.

Finally, who are the young people who believe in good, love and chance? They are concerned with politics, they do not see themselves as a marginal group, they live in the capital and in large towns, they are highly educated, women mainly. Part of the beliefs of young people reproduce ideological formulae. Belief in common sense is one of the ideological formulae advocated by the socialists; belief in general human values is part of the strategy of the Union of Democratic Forces.

Certainly, what matters in beliefs is not ideological formulae, but attitudes to the future; and here we find young people divided into extreme sceptics and pragmatic optimists.

PART IV

CONCLUSIONS

13 Prioritising youth in Russia: An investment for the future

IGOR ILYNSKY

Introduction

The proceeding chapters have set out a number of fundamental conclusions that present an extremely broad canvas portraying the development and current position of youth. They have also posed quite a few 'general' questions, such as: How may we describe in overall terms the current state of youth? Is it good or bad? Is it better or worse than previous younger generations? How is youth likely to behave in the immediate future? Is there a likelihood of some sort of spontaneous rebellion about which we hear so much today in the mass media? What should be the criteria by which we judge young people today and, consequently, what should they be striving for? What ideas should comprise the nucleus of a philosophy of a new youth policy?

Responses to these and similar questions cannot be identical. Social processes in Russia the CIS and East Central Europe are exceedingly complex and tangled; so their evaluation has to be multiple even when we are talking of the past. It is even more difficult to claim precision in assessing the present as we are unable to distance ourselves from events. And to forecast the future is a thankless task, even though it is one that is necessary and inevitable. This book is intended to facilitate the search for an answer to the fundamental question: What future awaits Russia and the other former communist states given *the young people it has now?* and given those trends and processes in the youth milieu that we have described? The link between the concepts 'youth' and 'future', 'social development' and 'youth development' is obvious. Youth is the same as society. Society is worthy of the youth it has. Youth is the future of society, the future society. Such postulates are hackneyed and banal. All the same ...

Negative social processes are not fatal. Life will ultimately exact its own price sooner or later, and the positive will somehow win through. But do we in Russia (or other ex-communist countries) have to wait until everything takes shape all by itself? We can surely *change* things for the better. Before we can, however, we have to understand what the state of affairs actually is; we must realise many of the negative processes and trends among young people will be irreversible unless we consciously set limits, unless we act to halt the course of events. If we do not, Russia can expect a global social catastrophe. Of course, at worse Russia will still have a future. Russia will continue to exist even if it disintegrates into numerous parts; some remaining section will bear the name *Rossiya* (Russia). ... It will just not be a great, strong and proud Russia. It will be a geographically small Russia, with insignificant material resources and a paltry population consisting of people who are unhealthy, physically and mentally un-developed. A Russia with a worthless economic, intellectual and cultural potential. Weak, dependent, with bitter thoughts of past grandeur and an inferiority complex about its present. If we are to look the truth fair and square in the face, we have to admit that it is a likely scenario for the future.

The origins of the youth crisis

It is important to realise that the problems this book has mentioned are the result of trends that began long ago, they are of a cumulative nature, they have turned from trends into some sort of 'negative' laws of life in society which 'operate' not for development, not for progress, but against them - for the destruction of the state, society, people and nation.

As research demonstrates, each successive generation of Russian youth is worse than the proceeding one in the basic indicators of social status and development. It is physically less healthy, mentally less developed, less spiritual and cultured, more amoral and criminal. It relates worse to work, is estranged from knowledge and education, from politics, from society and the state. The conclusion inevitably arises: the Russian people, the Russian nation is degenerating, slowly dying. This tragic resume runs counter to the proud Russian spirit, for it is hurtful and humiliating, it sounds like a criminal sentence.

This conclusion is not normally perceived in Russia because of the closed nature of social processes, their extension in time over decades and centuries, which make them go unnoticed and appear unremarkable. Yet facts and figures, many of them presented in preceding chapters, lead us to no other interpretation. Moreover, this situation has been exacerbated by the circumstances of recent years, accelerating, strengthening and aggravating all the prevalent negative processes, giving them a collapsing character. New trends have arisen; their scope is swiftly extending: marginalisation, forced migration, nationalism, religious fundamentalism, prostitution, crime and drug taking. All this means that, in its considerations on youth as a 'hope and support' for the economic and political reforms underway, society should not flatter itself too much: the possibilities and creative potential of young people (health, intellectual development, quality of knowledge, vocational training, attitude to work and to change in general, level of social activity, value orientations, etc.) far from correspond to those complex demands and tasks which need resolving for the successful transformation of post-totalitarian society. Nobody can tell just how great these 'scissors' are, but the fact that they exist and are great is an incontrovertible fact. What is more, analysis enables us to forecast the high probability of a 'youth rebellion' unless the negative trends are halted. In turn, a spontaneous youth explosion may become the detonator of mass popular actions that could bury for a long time all the hope for the future, including personal aspirations for a better society.

Defining the nature of the youth problem and appropriate responses

For a start we would need to find an exact definition of the task we have to carry out in order to correct the situation among young people and to lead Russia and the other ex-communist countries out of crisis. The commonplace term today is 'revival' whose essence consists in implementing change from the 'bad' present to the 'good' future, using pointers taken out of the pre-1917 past in Russia; they are very vulnerable and, in our view, completely unacceptable. It goes without saying that Russia has had great attainments in its history and they should be treasured. But to create new life on old canons is like constructing a spaceship from a steam-engine blueprint. Old Russia should not be glorified. The start of the present critical situation should be sought not merely in Russia's modern history, when for almost 80 years there was a coercive affirmation of the 'socialist way of life' and the 'formation of the new person'; it should be sought deep in the past. The servile psychology, drunkenness, bureaucracy and many other attributes that do nothing to enhance the Russian nation, only grew stronger in an atmosphere of socialist fear and mendacity; but they did not arise under socialism. We should also take account of the extra-ideological adverse consequences of scientific and technological progress and urbanisation.

Russia is sick, the foundations of her life and her organism have been undermined and, in many ways, destroyed. The people are poor. As a consequence, Russia needs not 'reviving', but 'rendering healthy', its life needs 'rearranging', to use Solzhenitsyn's term. This is a task that cannot be done quickly, by 'surgical' means. We can only use 'therapeutic' methods. Russia's way out of its critical state, its physical, intellectual, spiritual-moral, economic and political healing will take a historically lengthy period of time which will be shorter or longer depending upon how competent and intensive the 'treatment' will be. What is clear is the following:

1   Any ideas about a swift exit from the crisis constitute pure political adventurism;

2   The healing of the nation can take place only through the healing and development of new generations of Russians - children and young people;

3   (by dint of the first two circumstances), the current socio-economic reforms and all their specific programmes must be oriented on the future, 'tied to' young people who must, however, be not so much the object of upbringing and education, but *conscious participants* in social transformation and

4   The crisis in Russia (owing to its particular place in the world) is of a
     global nature linked to world development; consequently any exit from
     the crisis without taking into account world events and experience and
     without the help of the world community, is impossible: the proponents
     of national exclusivity, 'relying only on our own efforts', are doomed to
     failure. Russia can tear itself out of the vice of need only by following
     in the wake of the leading nations; it will be able to join them on the
     same level and then become a leading nation so long as the basis of its
     present reforms and progress will comprise theoretically and morally
     fully justified ideas, on the one hand a flexible scheme for social,
     political and economic change that conforms to the traditions of
     national life and level of development of Russian society; on the other
     Russia is being taken along the correct path 'in general', but along the
     wrong path in extremely essential 'particulars'.

The neglect of human resources in the transition period

A gross mistake being made by the proponents of reform, an error of
strategic importance, is that the reform concept is applied exclusively to the
economy, to implementing a market mechanism, privatisation and the
restructuring of the financial system. What they neglect is that the crisis of
Russian society is all-embracing and, therefore, cannot be overcome by
reforming just one aspect of social life - in this case, the economy. The
reformers are prisoners of historical economism, vulgar materialism; they
are actually operating as Marxists although they talk of freedom and
democracy, and are building a 'market economy'. The fact that human
beings are the creators and principal bearers of the changes is, as before,
being ignored. The 'miracle' of the American economy, of which so much is
made, was constructed on a purely psychological and ideological basis, in a
particular ethical and religious atmosphere which sanctions capitalist profit
as a legitimate reward for individual ability and effort. Similarly, the
Japanese 'miracle', much admired by millions of people, has more of a
psychological, spiritual-ethical and human nature than a material-economic
basis: the use of the spiritual and intellectual attainments of other nations,
substantiated in scientific information and accompanied by high

industriousness, discipline and organisation of Japanese science.   The Americans and Japanese realised precisely what the Russians have yet to understand: no economy exists in isolation. *All* forms of human endeavour are present and operate in the economic process. The most important of factor in any 'economic foundation' is the *desire* and ability of people to build that foundation. The economic process and production are not the major value of life. The key element is human beings, the individual as a value in itself and the principle of all principles. This means that the most important task is education, upbringing, science, culture and the development of spiritual and moral values.

Yet it is precisely these spheres that have been under attack in the course of the economic reform process, destroyed and forgotten since the collapse of communism in late 1991. The failure to appreciate that progress to a certain degree depends on social psychology, social consciousness, social morality and the political beliefs of millions of people, is holding back economic reform and inevitably putting an obstacle in their way unless the supremacy of the economy and production over all other spheres of life and over human beings themselves is reconsidered.

Involving the People in the reform process

The key, determining idea behind Russian reform and development should not simply be the creation of a 'new economic order' and the 'market economy' in themselves, divorced from human beings, it should be the *People* who understand the sense of the reform, who take part in it, expecting personal gain from it, at least in the foreseeable future. An appreciation of the new role of the human factor in development should today become the fundamental characteristic of the new political thinking of the 1990s. One must bear in mind that the main form of accumulation of *social wealth is largely the accumulation of new knowledge and other useful information - whose bearers are human beings - not of things, of finance capital and even not experience and habit.* It is the new forms of accumulation of social wealth (knowledge, information, talent, creativity - of intellectual, creative potential) that are the basic pre-requisites for progress and faster rates of social development. The direction, content and nature of the historical process increasingly depend not so much on material factors (geopolitical data, development of the means of production) as on human will (both individually and collectively), on the reaction of this will and mind to the emerging tasks of social life.

The difficulty consists not in once more pronouncing this viewpoint, but in taking human beings as our point of departure in the philosophy of Russian development, and from this point building the ideology of reforms in all its remaining parts. It is an exceptionally complicated task. Traditionally, both 'communist' and 'bourgeois' thinking present social conditions as the result of economic development, while the People are the *product* of those conditions to which human beings are subordinated like external, impotent factors. Naturally, in such circumstances, the people are the hostage and victim of economic, social and political conditions and circumstances.

Today we are witnessing the consequences of that philosophy of development. If we are to tackle the entire set of tasks of social development we must ultimately create in Russia a new type of culture that includes a renewed understanding of life, a renewed system of spiritual and moral values. We should complete the transition from primarily economic, material and nationalist values to internationalist, humane and spiritual values. In order to change society and nature, human beings must change themselves in the course of *humanist reform.* Nations and peoples, individuals, must learn to determine their own sovereignty and attain self-realisation not at the expense of others, but in the form of self-determination, sometimes through self-restraint. This philosophy of life must find a way to the social consciousness of Russian society.

A humanist reform programme

To carry out humanist reform is a global and therefore long-term task; it is addressed to the future, to future generations. At the centre of attention of current Russian domestic policy should therefore be not simply human beings in general, but young people as the bearers of the future in particular, as the vital source of innovation and the principal factor of change. Human beings and above all young people should today be the main area for financial, material and spiritual investment.

Russians cannot allow a policy intended to gain immediate profit without thinking about the consequences of a particular action for their future. To invest in the development of youth is to invest in the future of Russia. The time has come to talk of a principally new discovery of youth, the main prospect of which is to turn the spotlight on young people as the most valuable component in transforming society; youth is the most valuable period in human life for this task, in so far as it is then that people aspire for self-determination, self-affirmation, self-development and self-realisation. Youth is a particular type of value, it is society's vital element; it is not simply a demographic, but also an economic, social and political value. Such an approach to assessing youth, the stake of youth in the present, on the future generation, is capable of engendering a society and state policy working to control processes, to outstrip events, to provide therapy for phenomena, to accelerate development, instead of a policy of belated reaction to contradictions and problems already underway. In turn, this would enable us to carry through *accelerated* development, to *take* Russia into the forefront of social progress.

Putting young people first

'Stake on youth' does not mean creating some special conditions for it, augmenting the amount of state 'care' and 'aid', although in certain cases (disabled, young families, etc.) and in certain areas (education, upbringing, health, etc.), this is indeed needed. It is not a matter of rewarding consumerist, sponging attitudes among young people, which are obvious enough. The main objective is to unbridle youth - their thinking, creativity, energy and power, which today is mostly wasted or expended on affairs far from the needs, cares and tasks of society - in fact it is often opposed to society. *The integration, inclusion and participation* of youth in social life is the task about which state and social structures ought to be thinking. For young people to come to their senses and begin to act ('participate'), we need an appropriate *psychological* social atmosphere that would encourage them, appropriate *legal* pre-requisites, appropriate spiritual, moral and material *stimuli*.

Social ideal is of primary importance. We cannot count on rendering healthy Russian society and the Russian nation if we do not know where we are going, why and for what people are suffering and sacrificing themselves, for what *ultra*-individual goals life is worth living in Russia today. As a result of people's tendency towards self-deception and confusion, it frequently happens that entire peoples choose false values, distort and reject genuine values, set off on false historical trails and commit catastrophic errors, through which states and peoples themselves perish.

The history of humankind is full of such examples; the closest of them is the demise of the fascist and socialist states in the twentieth century and the incredible sufferings of their peoples. Having blundered in history, the older generations of Russia have left young people without a social ideal; yet they are doing nothing, even today, to elaborate this ideal; they pull young people in different directions, summoning them to follow, even though they have not the slightest idea where they themselves are going. In social life the plan always precedes production, the draft comes before construction, social ideas before the formation of socio-political systems in any social structure. The confusion of prospects at this time of great uncertainty is fraught with enormous danger for Russia in producing a new mistake in choosing a historical road, in producing a fresh wandering about the byways of history.

It was not so long ago that an ideology dominated the minds of millions of Russians; according to that set of ideas (Marxism-Leninism) the meaning of the natural and social sciences consisted in exposing the laws of development of nature and society with the purpose of employing them for human benefit. On that premise, we built the sermon and policy of self-confident pathos, one that would change the world; it proposed an *artificially* projected, modelled and 'scientifically created society' and it encapsulated the idea of shaping a 'new person'. In the final count, it brought humankind and Russia, in particular, to the brink of social catastrophe.

At the present time, Russian social consciousness has seized upon the diametrically opposed idea; that people should follow the *natural* (by which is actually meant something even worse - elemental) laws of nature and society (particularly and primarily in the economy) as the supreme manifestation of wisdom. In actual fact, what is being affirmed is that humankind is going forward to the future by groping around in the dark, without any possibility of saying something specific about it; what is more, it is not at all clear if people have any future at all. That the successes of 'natural' (read 'capitalist') society are considerably more imposing and the type of historical development today is evidently more preferable to 'scientifically created' society appears to be obvious to all - as also is the fact that the society is far from ideal. It may be better but it is not necessarily good. Even in highly developed countries there are marked flaws and vices, especially in the area of spirituality and culture. A sense of historical rupture, of the entry of humankind into some new phase of development with still vague outlines and alternatives, is growing in the social consciousness of Russia and the other post-communist Eastern European countries; ideas of the need for their own 'perestroika's' are at large.

Future paths of development

What road should Russia take? There is no clear answer. Cast on the whim of fate, young people are seeking an ideal independently. For most of them money has become their raison d'être and an end in itself; their ideal of the future is a Russia in which people have *lots* of money and *lots* of material things. It is easy to explain this view of life and society in the current situation, but one cannot agree that this vision can be an ideal of Russian history, the purpose of progress. As the history of all developed countries (USA, Japan, Germany, France) indicates, the consumer society is not simply an abundance of goods and services; it contains an acute shortage of spirituality, a poverty of morality, a paucity of cultural needs that put a brake on progress. Why should we take the path on which others have encountered spiritual and moral defeat and which also does not lead to the sacred temple?

Russia's social ideal is not likely to take shape quickly. It cannot be thought up, hatched out in scientific laboratories and presented to society. The ideal of Russian society is taking shape in the course of its development and the historical process, which is the result of the actions of the free will of individuals and communities freely selecting the dominant values of personal life and social development, and embodying them in their own creative endeavour. Russia's escape from crisis decisively depends on *what value will predominate*, become supreme in the life of society and, consequently, what will be the overall direction of the historical process and, depending on that, how other, including individual personal values will be perceived and become embodied in society.

Young people's right to choose

Renunciation of the erstwhile state and society does not yet provide a guarantee of a correct historical choice; every nation and every people have their own peculiarities which, irrespective of the overall direction of human development, predetermine their own special path in history. Young people are making a historical choice. This choice must be free, otherwise it is not a choice at all. But even if the choice is free, we must remember that freedom itself is not absolute. Young people must choose what they *have to* choose. The choice must not be haphazard, let alone erroneous. Only those goals which society recognises as *valuable* must prevail. *The system of new values must be the cornerstone of Russian reforms.* Only that which the individual, the people and society actually believe in and actually value can be made a reality.

Each nation, each society has its own system of values to which it aspires, which it 'cultivates' and out of which grows its culture. Russia's tragedy is that false values lay behind the life of its people for decades, even though they were proclaimed to be true and supreme. Socialism was thought to provide a very wide choice of all possible means of action without truly real goals of culture and moral restrictions. Without values to which these means were to be subordinated, rather than dominating over them, one could not reject, stifle or replace them. They were FREEDOM, JUSTICE, SOLIDARITY. They were HUMANISM, GOODNESS, HAPPINESS. They were the INDIVIDUAL, PEOPLE, NATION. They were SCIENCE, LITERATURE AND THE ARTS. They were FAMILY and HEALTH. They were CULTURE. They were HUMAN BEINGS who grew smaller in their virtues in their own eyes and had to be elevated. They were INDIVIDUALITY. It is not enough to change the external material and social conditions of the life and development of youth, one must change the internal structure of the individual. The reforms should take place mainly within young people themselves, not over and around them. Where there is a bad individual there is also a bad society.

FREEDOM is the supreme spiritual premise of society from which grows the entire set of values that lead people to the heights of self-determination and self-development. The whole hierarchy and system of values of Russian democratic society and the younger generation must be built on the postulate of the priority of freedom as the supreme value.

The *set of values* of the new Russia will not take root all at once. Nor will people understand straightaway what is 'good'. Goodness often wears modest attire. On the other hand, frequently objective evil is subjectively perceived as goodness or a blessing, since it wears the mask of good. We are building hydro-electric and nuclear power stations, and we talk of the advantages they bring, yet we do not wish to see the terrible consequences of their operations on the environment, on the air we breathe or the water we drink. We launch conflicts and wars for 'the people's good' - and kill them in doing so. And so on. That is why, before positive values can take root in the minds of Russian youth, they must have an understanding of 'what is bad', what they must *not* do under any circumstances. The conduct, deeds and actions of young people must be tied in with certain moral imperatives (injunctions, requirements) *of Russian history* without following which both Russia and its youth can have no future.

The ecological imperative means unswervingly observing certain conditions and restrictions which harmonise the needs of Russian society and people with the opportunities that nature can still provide. Russia needs a new ethical attitude to its flora and fauna, and use of material resources. The Russian citizen should take pride in being thrifty and economical, and not being wasteful; the citizen's attitude towards the environment must be based on an understanding of the harmony of nature, and not the idea of conquering it - a conception that the old regime tried to instil for decades.

Russians must subordinate their activity to a set of rules and regulations which have yet to be defined. We should give back to the Russian the religious sense of constant concern about whether he has yielded to the eternal instead of the immediate, whether he has lost a sense of finiteness of his being, an awareness of an imminent global threat. Of course, the principles and restrictions in relations with nature are bound to change as Russian science develops, as we improve the technological basis of the Russian economy. But first they have to be understood and accepted by Russian society and its younger generation as one of the highest forms of morality. Russian society has to cultivate an attitude to nature as a supreme value comparable only with that of human life. Nature is life. Ecology is a sphere in which the youth of Russia must display their intelligence, energy, will and responsibility. IT is a pressing task to form a mass ecological youth movement. Ecological education and upbringing must be part of the school and university curriculum, part of everyday life, in the programmes of political parties and youth organisations. Young people must know and understand that the ecological situation in Russia is just about the worst in the world; if it is not improved, if it continues to deteriorate, all talk of the future is worthless; Russia and its population can only expect physical extermination.

The imperative of concord and peace. The minds of Russian citizens for decades had instilled in them the Marxist thesis that the source of development was to be found in the internal contradictions of everything living. The law of dialectics on unity and struggle of opposites philosophically justified the source of motion and development of the world process, class struggle and social revolution. The logic of class struggle gave birth to the philosophy of class hatred which was tenaciously cultivated and penetrated all areas of Soviet society and its policy, including the international sphere. The fighting psychology, the fighting spirit of Russians which was encouraged and successfully formed as a vital feature of the 'new person', still today continues its dubious service - the Chechen crisis. Russian society is historically in conflict, by definition. Russians have been taught to seek out enemies and prepare for war and struggle. Concepts of harmony and concord, solidarity, dialogue and consensus are only now starting to enter youth consciousness.

At the same time, circumstances are provoking and encouraging aggression, radicalism, maximalism and extremism. The danger of a social explosion, including a youth explosion, is very real. Russia is already drawn into conflicts on the territory of the former USSR. Russia itself is fraught with conflicts for numerous reasons. Russian society needs a strong principle of social harmony, toleration, community and peace. Everyone is interested in this principle, especially youth. It is in the fire of war and conflict that above all young people perish (see Chapter 9). For war and conflict turn their future into something to fear and into unfulfilled hopes. The thesis of struggle must be removed from the young mind and replaced by the principle of harmony, concord and peace. We must never more extol war and revolution as ways of resolving contradictions. Every war and struggle always comes to an end. Even if the aim of war is not satisfied, it still comes to an end. For a 'war to a victorious finish' consumes those involved and threatens to extinguish the combatants. The principle of harmony, concord and peace outweighs in its humaneness the principle of antagonism, struggle and war.   Every war ultimately has a striving for peace. War is for the sake of peace, and not peace for the sake of war. It was Heraclitus who said that 'a marvellous harmony is born out of opposites'. Out of opposites and not out of identity, not out of unison. The contradictory and incompatible in social life remains irreconcilable, disputable, hateful, struggling and combatant until agreement can be found. For the time being, there is no desire to find agreement. When this desire and aspiration can be found, then we have an opportunity to commence a dialogue so as to turn the inimical-incompatible into amical-agreeable - to establish harmony. The entire system of education and social upbringing in Russia, the activity of the Church, youth organisations and the mass media must be aimed at educating future generations in a spirit of peace, friendship and co-operation among people, nations and states, at forming an atmosphere of tolerance and accord.   Peace is one of the highest values whose neglect can threaten both human and social life.

Promoting Russian unity

The imperative of unity of the Russian nation. The Russian nation - an inimitable phenomenon in its uniqueness - is a close-knit family of many peoples and nations that has come together historically and formed a consciousness over many centuries of historical destiny, forming a community of state, cultural and economic interests. The vitality of the Russian nation has been tried and tested by history. Today, however, the unity of the Russian nation is under threat. The major among many reasons for that is *nationalism* taken to the extreme, to hatred and contempt for other nations, to the ideas of superiority, the forced attachment or conquest of other peoples, and the *ambitions of political leaders* exploiting national feeling for the sake of gaining power and achieving their ambitious designs.

Russia is not simply a common territory; the people of Russia are not simply a sum total of peoples living on this territory.   Russia is an association of many nationalities and peoples. It is an organic association. It is a complex association. It is a unity and integral formation. Russia is a *complex, organically uniform nation.*   The political and cultural development, national self-awareness and state traditions of some peoples who are part of Russia permit us to put them in the category of nation. In that sense, their desire for independence is natural. The human need creatively to serve one's people, one's nation, the conscious desire to uncover their creative forces, to affirm one's people and one's nation among other peoples and nations can only be welcomed; serving humankind can only be done through the nation. Yet this does not remove the organic adherence of a people-nation to a more intricate, primary formation - to the Russian nation. The nations, peoples and nationalities of Russia are welded together by a common language, culture and spiritual aspirations, state and economic interests, a common historical past and, most important of all, a united aspiration for the future - to make Russia a free, democratic and flourishing country. The nations, peoples and nationalities of Russia unify in a single whole a strong national feeling - love for the historical aspect and creativity of the Russian nation, a faith in its particular historical mission and desire for the creative flourishing of Russia. Together the peoples of Russia will overcome all the difficulties of their development; living apart will bring them fresh and protracted sufferings. Love of Russians for Russia, faith in Russia and a desire to maintain its unity are all guarantees for the recovery, animation and grandeur of Russia.

Young people have to appreciate that the existence of a strong and great Russia corresponds to the fundamental and long-term interests of the younger generation; and that can only happen if the nation remains united. Young people must resist the desire of ambitious power-seekers to use them as an instrument for satisfying their own ambitious ends, which can only result in the downfall of Russia. They must launch an all-Russia movement to maintain the national integrity of Russia under such slogans as 'National chauvinism will not pass!' or 'For a united and undivided Russia!'.

Devising a new youth policy for Russia

The imperative of a youth policy. Reform proponents had thought it possible to ignore the youth factor, to parenthesise their youth policy with its needs and interests, preferring not to think about a youth policy at all; they did so by counting on a 'swift' variant of considered 'reform from above', allowing through that tactic the opportunity for narrowing the social basis of the reforms. In essence, the reform support was no more than patience, naive faith and an illusion of the people. The 'blitz reform' did not succeed.

Patience ran out and the illusions were once more dispelled. The people no longer believe anyone but themselves. The reforms can no longer continue 'above' the people, against their will. We see a swift radicalisation of popular attitudes which can in the immediate future reach extreme forms. In that situation, the President, parliament and government will not be able to continue their governing functions under the old regime. If they want to survive and act *for the continuation of reform*, they must at once concern themselves with creating the widest possible social basis for their policy. That means an alliance with political parties and blocs, with trade unions and youth organisations, with young people as a whole. The authorities cannot conduct merely tactical games, propound a philosophy of time-servers and behave themselves as time-servers, even being such in reality. A civic responsibility to their country, honour and conscience should compel them to think of the future, to bring their tactical actions in line with the strategy of Russia's development, *to search for, find and do everything in their power to nurture the shoots of its future growth* which are to be found mainly amongst the young. A stake on youth is inevitable, it has to be made sooner or later. That is a condition of retaining at least transparent social stability and the course of reform. The current extremely critical situation requires an immediate start to the construction in Russia of an effective youth policy for including the innovatory, creative potential of young people in tackling general national problems.

The process of forming a state youth policy and the strategic objectives of such a policy should be based on the demands and possibilities of the new social conditions in which society and young people find themselves, the requirements and interests of young people, the needs and interests of society in the normal social development of the younger generation. In this connection *what we need is a re-orientation and clarification of the conceptual nucleus of a philosophy of a modern youth policy* through reinforcing the focus in some directions and weakening it in others.

Acceleration of the social development of the younger generation as the decisive condition for Russia's *accelerated* rescue from its crisis is the key innovatory element of a youth policy at the current stage of Russia's development (all-embracing crisis in society, degeneration of the nation, etc.).

Proceeding from that, the *main aim* of a Russian youth policy is to establish the necessary *social conditions* for promoting youth through mass state and public support for innovative activity, the *social protection* of youth, the formation of its creative endeavour, talents and habits, as well as *stimuli* to help its self-development and self-realisation through which we can create the prerequisites for its accelerated development. Youth policy must reflect both the common requirements of all young people and the needs of its various social and age groups while taking into account the specific conditions of different regions and localities.

There must be a considerable shift away from efforts which for many years were intended primarily *to shape, educate and socialise* young people; we must now move to *restructuring society itself, removing in it elements of irrationality and social injustice with regard to the younger generation.* In order to adapt (accommodate) young people to a society that lacks a clear social ideal and a stable set of values, society must take a step towards young people, adapt itself (accommodate itself) to them. In other words, socialisation of youth must simultaneously take place alongside the rejuvenation of society through the inculcation into the social consciousness of ideas, views, premises and values of young people, the highest models of youth culture.

Future directions

The sphere of youth policy must contain priority orientations and sectors. They can be singled out while elaborating a complex programme on 'Youth and Russia in the twenty-first century' which must be ratified by President and parliament as both a state and all-society affair.

One of the priorities of youth policy should be the formation of a new socio-state system of *civic education* of young people so as to enable them more intensively and profoundly to master the ideals and values of a free, democratic Russia. A crucial criterion of a young person's education must be his or her *participation* in social life on a voluntary basis, while the supreme indicator should be the ability to *serve* Russia, to live for one's country as well as for oneself and one's nearest and dearest. The idea of patriotic *service* to Russia should become the core of state and social education, the formation of spiritual and moral values cementing the Russian nation into a single entity.

Youth policy should be of *a differentiated nature*. Differentiation occurs, firstly, in various *directions*: new policies should be implemented in education, upbringing, vocational training, employment, health and social provision.   These policies are to be put into practice by special state ministries, departments and structures with public participation.   Youth policy must also differentiate *by level* of implementation. The complexity and uniqueness in Russian regional development precludes any chance of applying a unified model and its direct translation into incompatible conditions and tasks. Youth policy must have its own interpretation for each republic, region and locality.

At the same time, it must also possess an *integrative character*.   Its integration stems from an appreciation of the new social realities in which Russia now finds herself. We need to work out a joint strategy for survival and development of all republics and regions concerning youth. Within the framework of national co-operation, it is important to develop concerted action aimed at resolving the following tasks: to ensure that the central authorities implement more radical measures and policies in tackling national youth problems; to support the actions of various state structures and public organisations in safeguarding the rights of young people and finally attempts must be made to improve opportunities for establishing the fundamentals of formulating a sensible model for a balanced youth policy.

Youth policy itself is becoming the principal instigator of efforts by state and public structures in the area of youth; it is lending to their efforts a *common vision, an integral nature, a non-contradictoriness, thereby serving to enhance the effectiveness of these measures.*

Some conclusions

What is evident in Russia and throughout Eastern Europe is the need for co-ordinated and extensive action at a national level aimed at combining efforts, joint creative endeavour and converting the differences between the parties involved into a stimulating impulse for co-operation, the mutual enrichment of youth policy through exchange of experience between the regions and various spheres of activity.   What is also apparent is the need for appropriate selection of strictly differentiated approaches, policies, measures and programmes, effectively reflecting youth needs on both national and regional levels in accordance with local conditions.

Youth policy in Russia and in other post-communist regimes of Eastern Europe should not be left purely to the state, although state policy will be of primary importance given existing conditions. An important component of youth policy should be the social element, representing the activity of a broad alliance of various types of youth associations and organisations as well as numerous social structures acting in the interests of young people. The international youth organisations of Russia could act as the initiators and major co-ordinators of a 'Youth of the World to the Youth of Russia' movement.

Conclusions

Starting from the premise that youth was a potential problem area for society the former Soviet Union (FSU) and East-Central European (ECE) states sought to exert control over young people's lives. One of the most important ways to achieve this was through the *Komsomol* or its corresponding organisations in the various East European countries. These youth organisations created a false dichotomy in which it appeared that youth was a prioritised group under 'state socialism', when in fact the opposite was true: it was largely powerless, in so far as youth organisations were under party-state control.

As many of the contributors show, only officially sanctioned youth activity and behaviour was permissible up to 1985 in the case of the FSU and prior to 1989 in the case of ECE. The outcome was that young people were excluded from the political process. Not surprisingly, therefore, young people were in the forefront of the 1989 revolutions throughout ECE, and also as members of the various national movements they undermined Soviet legitimacy which led to the collapse of the USSR in late 1991.

The questions which this book has attempted to answer are as follows: what has happened to young people in the post-communist phase? what do they think about politics now? how are the post-communist regimes responding to the problems of youth in the transition to a market economy? and finally, should the FSU and ECE follow the West in trying to resolve the 'youth crisis'?

With regard to the first of these questions, young people appear to be disillusioned and apathetic and feel neglected by the state and political parties. They have been adversely affected by the economic and political reform process and do not see the post-communist regimes as their salvation, but instead rely more on family and friends. However in some countries, such as Slovakia, as Machacek illustrated, young people are fighting back by organising their own self-help and other youth organisations run in the interests of youth. In the main, young people are only interested in money and have largely turned their back on religion, respect for authority and also embark upon criminal activity in order to survive. They constitute the neglected section of the population.

Although young people played a key role in toppling the communist regimes in ECE and the FSU, since 1989 and 1991 respectively, and the demise of official youth organisations, they are no longer represented in any real sense by the state or political parties. State youth policy and youth lobbying through political parties have fallen victim to the economic and political instability in Russia and elsewhere, on the one hand, and to the fragmentation and weak nature of existing political parties and parliaments, on the other. Several contributors clearly demonstrate that young people have little or no interest in politics, do not want to participate in the political process and have no faith in the ability of politicians to solve their everyday concerns - education, jobs, an uncertain future. They are also highly dissatisfied with the direction and speed of the transition.

Although the main reason for the poor state response is in overcoming half a century of totalitarianism, the various post-communist regimes are also to blame for failing to prioritise youth policy. They have failed to take the necessary steps to reverse what Igor Ilynsky refers to as the 'crisis in values'. The post-communist states have continued past rhetoric about declining morality, materialism, the brain drain, etc. But this is only words not action. State policies have lacked coherence and government officials have by and large failed to consult young people themselves. Moreover, government agencies, such as the State Committee for Youth in Russia, lack sufficient political clout and resources to get the job done. As a consequence, the state has failed to reverse the widespread pessimism among youth and there appears to be a general feeling among all the contributors that today's young people in the FSU and ECE countries might sadly become the 'lost' or 'forgotten generation'.

The collapse of communism led to the destruction of traditional youth values - respect for the state, equality, internationalism, collectivism, love for one's fellow wo/man, etc. - but they have not been replaced by easily identifiable new values. There is currently a large vacuum in which young people believe in themselves (individualism), family, money and to a lesser extent in the value of education, religion and politics. In the short term, this void has been filled in some cases by extremism and a nationalist orientation (former DDR); in others by a belief in one's country (Belorus) and in yet other instances this situation has engendered a national identity crisis (Russia; former Yugoslavia).

At present, this has meant that young people are alienated from the political system, most countries of the FSU and ECE have no civic culture, there is little sense of community (this is more the case in Russia than Belorus) and political participation is low. The post-communist leaderships have therefore failed to fulfil the promises they made to youth in 1989 in the case of ECE and since 1991 in the case of the FSU, that they would be provided with a better, more secure future once the communist edifice had gone.

A continuation of a situation in which youth policy is given insufficient attention and not taken seriously enough, on the hand, and in which young people are not involved in policy and decision-making during the transition from totalitarianism to liberal democracy, on the other, is likely to undermine and possibly prove a long-term obstacle to a successful transformation of the economic and political systems of the FSU and ECE.

Is unification and world integration the solution? Most contributors from the East suggest that a more concerted, systematic state response is required to help young people to overcome their difficulties in the transition period. Can the West help Russia and the other countries find a solution to current youth ills?

There are two possible approaches here: firstly, many post-totalitarian regimes of the FSU and ECE argue that they must learn to solve their own youth problems in their own way. This means rejecting Western solutions as inappropriate. Second, there is the opposing view that many of the problems of Russian and East European youth described in this book have existed in the West for decades, so we can help each other overcome them. This necessitates Russia and other countries moving closer to the West. In this sense, therefore, the difficulties facing young people are the product of the modernisation process and the transition to a market economy and pluralist political system. Thus, once a successful transition has been made, current teething problems will be quickly overcome. But just how long will transition take? Several decades as in the case of Spain and Portugal or longer, perhaps an entire generation? and how long can we expect young people to wait?

There are already signs, in Russia at least since the December 1993 elections, that time is running out. These elections indicated that there was a desire for 'a strong order', no trust in existing political leaders and a possible backlash by the neo-fascists, communists and nationalists to combat the destruction of traditional values, especially patriotism and the national ideal, in order to avert further state collapse. Some young people were behind Zhirinovsky's (neo-fascist) Liberal Democratic Party. Similar trends, as Hennig shows, have been happening in the Eastern part of Germany since 1989. These have been echoed in other ECE countries too, where many young people have joined neo-fascist groups.[1]

This book describes the current situation in several countries of the FSU and ECE. As a result, readers should now be aware of the extent and nature of the youth problem and national governments and advisers should also know what should *not* be done - a repeat of past mistakes in the Soviet period. Several contributions indicate what is required in order to halt adverse developments - a more active state role, a more positive perception of youth with an emphasis on their potential; the need to prioritise youth as an investment for the future and finally there is a need for the state to act as a stabilising factor in the transition period. This has been extremely difficult to achieve in most cases, but especially in war-torn Yugoslavia. The implementation of a successful state youth policy will depend on many factors, the key one being whether the reforms continue to be perceived by young people, and adults alike, as destructive rather than constructive. Either way the FSU and various ECE countries cannot allow the rapid decline in living standards, rising nationalism, emigration, ethnic conflict and crisis in national values among youth - the bed-rock of each country's future - to continue without long-term consequences for economic recovery and political stability. It would seem sensible for the various post-communist regimes to act now, in collaboration with Western colleagues and on equal terms, to address one of the most important issues of the late twentieth century - the youth crisis.

Note

1   On this see, for example, P. Hockenos, Free to Hate: *The Rise of the Right in Post-Communist Eastern Europe* (London, Routledge 1993).

Bibliography

Abrams, D. et al. (1990), 'AIDS invulnerability, relationships, sexual behaviour and attitudes among 16 to 19 year olds', in Aggleton, P. et al. (eds), *AIDS: Individual, cultural and policy dimensions*, Falmer Press, Lewes.

Abrams, M. (1959), *The Teenage Consumer*, Routledge & Kegan Paul, London.

Aggleton, P. (1993), 'Voluntary sector responses to HIV and AIDS: A framework for analysis', in Aggleton, P. et al. (eds), *AIDS: Facing the Second Decade*, Falmer Press, Lewes.

Alexeyev, A.A. et al. (1990), *Stroka v biografii Sekretarii Tsentralnovo Komiteta Komsomola, 1918-1990gg*, Moscow.

Anokhin, S. et al. (1989), *Ocherednoi krizis ili tupik (polemicheskie zametki o Komsomole)*, Moscow.

Armstrong, G. and Wilson, M. (1973), 'City politics and deviance amplification' in Taylor, I. and Taylor, L. *Politics and Deviance*, Penguin, Harmondsworth.

Attwood, L. (1990), *The New Soviet Man and Woman: Sex-role Socialisation in the USSR*, Macmillan, London.

Attwood, L. (1993), 'Sex and the cinema', in Kon, I. and Riordan, J. (eds), *Sex and Russian Society*, Pluto Press, London.

AIDS: Monitoring Response to the Public Education Campaign February 1986 - February 1987 (1987), HMSO, London.

AIDS Surveillance in the EC and Cost Countries (1993), European Centre for the Epidemiological monitoring of AIDS, Quarterly Report, France, March.

Aitkin, P.P. (1978), *Ten to Fourteen Year Olds and Alcohol*, HMSO, Edinburgh.

Bagnell, G. (1988), 'Use of alcohol, tobacco and illicit drugs amongst 13 year olds in three areas of Britain', *Drug and Alcohol Dependence*, 22.

Bagnell, G. (1991), 'Alcohol and drug use in a Scottish cohort: 10 years on', *British Journal of Addiction*, 86.

Becker, H. (1963), *Outsiders - Studies in the Sociology of Deviance*, Free Press, New York.

Binnie, H.L. and Murdock, G. (1969), 'The attitudes to drugs and drug takers of students of the University and colleges of higher education in an English Midland city', University of Leicester Vaughan Papers No. 14.

Box, S. (1981), *Deviance, Reality and Society*, Holt, Rinehart and Winston, New York.

Brake, M. (1980), *The Sociology of Youth Culture and Youth Subcultures*, Routledge & Kegan Paul, London.

Brake, M. (1985), *Comparative Youth Culture*, Routledge & Kegan Paul, London.

Brown, C. and Lawton, J. (1988), *Illicit Drug Use in Portsmouth and Havant*, Policy Studies Institute, London.

Buckley, M. (1992), 'Social change and Social Policy', in White, S. et al. (eds), *Developments in Soviet and post-Soviet Politics*, Macmillan, London.

Bushnell, J. (1990), *Moscow Graffiti: Language and Subculture*, Unwin Hyman, London.

Calnan, M. (1973), 'The politics of health: the case of smoking control', *Journal of Social Policy,* Vol. 2, Part 3.

Carson, W.G. and Wyles, P. (1971), *Crime and Delinquency in Britain: Sociological Readings*, Martin Robertson, London.

Chambers, G. and Tombs, J. (eds) (1984), *The British Crime Survey*, HMSO, Edinburgh.

Chaika, N.A. (1991), 'Navstrechu sobstvennoi pogibeli', *Zdorov'e*, No. 3.

Chalidze, V. (1977), *Criminal Russia: Essays on Crime in the Soviet Union*, Random House, New York.

Cherednichenko, G. and Shubkin, B. (1985), *Youth is Coming*, Moscow.

Cloward, R. and Ohlin, L.E. (1955), *Delinquency and Opportunity*, Free Press, New York.

Cicourel, A.V. (1968), *The Social Organisation of Justice*, Wiley, New York.

Coggans, D. et al. (1989), *National Evaluation of Drug Addiction in Scotland*, Centre for Occupational and Health Psychology, University of Strathclyde.

Cohen, P. (1972), 'Subcultural conflict and working-class community', *Working Papers in Cultural Studies*, University of Birmingham No. 2.

Cohen, S. (1973), *Folk Devils and Moral Panics*, Paladin, London.

Coleman, J. (1980), 'Friendship and the peer group in adolescence', in Adelson, J. (ed), *Handbook of Adolescent Development*, Wiley, New York.

Comely, L. (1991), 'Lesbian and gay teenagers at school: how can educational psychologists help?', Paper presented to British Psychological Society conference, Bournemouth.

Conger, J. (1982), *Adolescence: A Generation Under Pressure*, Harper and Row, London.

Connor, W.D. (1972), *Deviance in Soviet Society: Crime, Delinquency and Alcoholism*, Columbia University Press, New York.

Cotsgrove, S. (Revised ed. 1973), *The Science of Society: An Introduction to Sociology*, Allen & Unwin, London.

Danshin, I. and Kokotov, M. (1968), 'Izuchenie prichin prestupnosti', *Sotsialisticheskoe zakonnost'*, No. 12.

Darling, C.A. et al. (1984), 'Sex in transition; 1900-1980', *Journal of Youth and Adolescence* 13.

Davies, J.B. and Stacey, B. (1972), *Teenagers and Alcohol: A Developmental Study in Glasgow*, HMSO, London.

Department of Transport (1990), *Road Accidents in Britain: The Casualty Report*, Government Statistical Office.

DiClemente, D. et al. (1986), 'Adolescents and AIDS: A survey of knowledge, attitudes and beliefs about AIDS in San Francisco', *American Journal of Public Health*, Vol. 76.

Dobson, R.B. (1991), 'Youth problems in the Soviet Union', in Jones, A. et al. (eds), *Soviet Social Problems*, Boulder, Westview Press.

Dossier 'Vybory - 90' (1990), Moscow.

Downes, D. (1966), *The Delinquent Solution*, Routledge & Kegan Paul, London.

Eisenstadt, S.N. (1965), *From Generation to Generation*, Free Press, Chicago.

Erikson, K.J. (1966), *Wayward Puritans*, Wiley, London.

Fish, F. et al. (1974), 'Prevalence of drug abuse amongst young people in Glasgow, 1970-1972', *British Journal of Addiction*, Vol. 69.

Fisher, R. (1959), *Pattern for Soviet Youth: A Study of the Congresses of the Komsomol, 1918-54*, Columbia University Press, New York.

Ford, N. (1990), 'Psycho-Active drug use, sexual activity and AIDS Awareness of young people in Bristol ', Institute of Population Studies, University of Exeter.

Ford, N. and Morgan, K. (1989), 'Heterosexual lifestyles of young people in an English city', *Journal of Population and Social Studies* Vol. 1.

Foreman, D. and Chilvers, C. (1989), 'Sexual behaviour of young and middle aged men in England and Wales', *British Medical Journal* 298.

Foster, K. et al. (1990), *General Household Survey 1988*, HMSO, London.

Freeman, R. (1992), 'The politics of Aids in Britain and Germany', in Aggleton, P. et al. (eds), *AIDS: Rights, Risks and Reason*, Falmer Press, Lewes.

Frith, S. (1984), *The Sociology of Youth*, Causeway Books, Ormskirk.

Fursev, V. (1968), 'Nekotorye voprosy sostoianiia i struktury prestupnosti nesovershennoletnykh v Kazakhstanskoi SSR', in: U Dzhekebaev (ed), *Voprosy bor'by s prestupnost'iu nesovershennoletnykh*, Nauka, Alma Ata.

Gelishchanov, A. (1979), 'Juvenile crime in the Georgian SSR', *Radio Liberty Research* 25/79.

Gertsenzon, A.A. (1960), 'The community's role in the prevention of crime', *Soviet Review* No. 1.

Ghodse, H. et al. (1985), 'Deaths of drug addicts in the United Kingdom, 1962-1981', *British Medical Journal* 320.

Goddard, E. (1990), *Why Children Start Smoking,* HMSO, London.

Goldman, R.J. and Golman, J.D.G. (1988), *Show Me Yours: Understanding Children's Sexuality*, Penguin, Ringwood.

Golod, I. (1969), 'Sociological problems of sexual morality', *Soviet Sociology* Vol. 13, No. 1, Summer.

Gonsiorek, J. (1988), 'Mental health issues of gay and lesbian adolescents', *Journal of Adolescent Health Care*, 9.

Goode, E. (1972), *Drugs in American Society*, Knopf, New York.

Gorbachov, M.S. (1989), *Molodezh - tvorcheskaya sila revolutionnogo obnoveleniya*, Moscow.

Griffin, C. (1988), 'Youth research: young women and the "gang of lads" model', in Hazekemp, J. et al. (eds), *European Contributions to Youth Research*, University of Amsterdam Press., Amsterdam.

Griffin, C. (1993), *Representations of Youth: The Study of Youth and Adolescence in Britain and America*, Polity Press, London.

Hall, S. and Jefferson, T. (1976), *Resistance through Rituals*, Hutchinson, London.

Harkin, A.M. and Hurley, M. (1988), 'National survey on public knowledge of AIDS in Ireland', *Health Education Research 3*.

Hawker, A. (1978), *Adolescents and Alcohol*, Edsall, London.

Hebidge, D. (1979), *Subculture: The Meaning of Style*, Methuen, London.

Hindess, B. (1973), *The Use of Official Statistics*, Macmillan, London.

Hockenos, P. (1993), *Free to Hate: The Rise of the Right in Post-Communist Eastern Europe*, Routledge, London.

Holland, J. et al. (1990), 'Don't die of ignorance - I nearly died of embarrassment' Condoms in Context, The Womens Risk AIDS Project, Paper No. 2, Tufnell Press, London.

Home Office (1990), *Offences of Drunkenness, England & Wales 1989*, Statistical Bulletin 40/90, Home Office, London.

Hough, M. and Mayhew, P. (1983), *The British Crime Survey*, HMSO, London.

Howitt, D. (1982), *The Mass Media and Social Problems*, Pergamon, Oxford.

Ikonnikova, S. (1974), *Youth*, Leningrad.

Ilynsky, I.M. and Sharonov, A.V. (eds.) (1993), *Molodoyozh Rossii. Tendentsii, perspektivy*, Moscow.

Iz Glubiny (1991), Moscow.

Jahoda, G. and Crammond, J. (1972), *Children and Alcohol: A Developmental Study in Glasgow*, HMSO, London.

Jeffery-Poulter, S. (1991), *Peers, Queers & Commons: The Struggle for Gay Law Reform from 1950 to the Present*, Routledge, London.

Juliver, P. (1976), *Revolutionary Law and Order: Politics and Social Change in the USSR*, Free Press, New York.

Kinsey, R. (1984), *The Merseyside Crime Survey*, Merseyside Metropolitan Council.

Kinsey, R. et al. (1986), *Losing the Fight*, Blackwell, Oxford.

Kirillov, I. (1991), 'Potreblenie alkogolia i sotsial'nye posledstviia p'ianstva i alkogolizma', *Vestnik Statistiki*, No. 6.

Kon, I. (1993), 'Sexuality and Culture' in Kon, I. and Riordan, J. (eds), *Sex and Russian Society*, Pluto Press, London.

Kosarev, A. (1963), *Sbornik vospominanii*, Moscow.

Kosviner, A. and Hawks, D. (1977), 'Cannabis use amongst British University students, II: Patterns of use attitudes of use', *British Journal of Addiction* 72.

Kozlov, A. and Lisovsky, V. (1986), *Young People: Formation of Modes of Life*, Moscow.

Kramer, J.M. (1988), 'Drug abuse in the USSR', *Problems of Communism*, March-April.

Kramer, J.M. (1990), 'Drug abuse in Eastern Europe: An emerging issue of public policy', *Slavic Review* Vol. 49, No. 1, Spring.

Kramer, J.M. (1991), 'Drug abuse in the USSR', in Jones, A. et al. (eds), *Soviet Social Problems*, Westview Press, Boulder.

Lemert, E. (1972), *Human Deviance, Social Problems and Social Control*, Prentice-Hall, New York.

Lenin, V.I. (1975), 'Internatsional molodyozhi', in Lenin, V.I., *Polnoe sobranie sochinenii*, Volume 30, Moscow.

Marsh, A. et al. (1986), *Adolescent Drinking*, HMSO, London.

Materialy XXI-ovo syezda VLKSM (1990), Moscow.

McKay, B. (1992), 'Communists meet to reform party youth wing', *Moscow Times* 21 April.

McKay, D. et al. (1973), 'Drug taking amongst medical students at Glasgow University', *British Medical Journal* 1.

McMurran, M. (1991), 'Young offenders and alcohol-related crime: what interventions will address the issues?', *Journal of Adolescence*, Vol. 14.

McRobbie, A. (1978), 'Working-class girls and the culture of femininity', in: Centre for Contemporary Cultural Studies (eds), *Women Take Issue*, Hutchinson, London.

Mays, J.B. (1965), *The Young Pretenders*, Michael Joseph, London.

Medvedev, R. (1972), *Let History Judge*, Macmillan, London.

Merton, R. (1938), 'Social structure and Anomie', *American Sociological Review*.

Miller, W.B. (1958), 'Lower class culture as a generating milieu of gang delinquency', *Journal of Social Issues* 15.

Mir Filosofii (1991), Part II, Moscow.

Moore, S. (1991), *Investigating Deviance*, Collins, London.

Moore, S. and Rosenthal, D. (1993), *Sexuality in Adolescence*, Routledge, London.

Moral Images of Soviet Youth (1985), Minsk.

Mott, J. (1989), 'Self-reported cannabis use in Great Britain in 1981', *British Journal of Addiction* 80.

Nagaev, V.V. (1971), 'Anketnoe issledovanie rasprostranennosti upotreblenia alkogol'nykh napitkov', *Zdravookhranenie Rossiskoi Federatsii*, No. 12.

Novgorodstev, P.I. (1991), *Ob obshchestvennom ideale*, Moscow.

Nutbeam, D. et al. (1989), 'Public knowledge and attitudes to AIDS', *Public Health* 103.

O Polozhenii v Komsomole i o putakh yevo vykhoda iz krizisa (1990), Moscow.

Organizatsionno-ustavnye voprosy komsomolskoi raboty (1973), Moscow.

Parker, H. et al. (1988), *Living with Heroin*, Open University Press, Milton Keynes.

Paschenkov, V.P. et al. (1972), *Nekotorye voprosy nasledstvennosti pri khronicheskom alkogolizme*, Meditsina, Moscow.

Pearson, G. (1983), *Hooligan: A History of Respectable Fears*, Macmillan, London.

Pervyi vserossisky syezd RKSM (1926), Moscow-Leningrad, 3rd edition.

Phillipson, M. (1971), *Sociological Aspects of Crime and Delinquency*, Routledge & Kegan Paul, London.

Pilkington, H. (1992), 'Whose space is it anyway? Youth, gender and civil society in the Soviet Union', in Rai, S. et al. (eds), *Women in the Face of Change: The Soviet Union, Eastern Europe and China*, Routledge., London.

Plant, M. (1973), 'Young people at risk: A study of the 17-24 age group', Cheltenham Youth Trust, Cheltenham.

Plant, M. and Plant, M. (1992), *Risk Takers: Alcohol, Drugs, Sex and Youth*, Routledge, London.

Plant, M.A. et al. (1985), *Alcohol, Drugs and School-leavers*, Tavistock, London.

Plummer, K. (1989), 'Lesbian and gay youth in England', *Journal of Homosexuality* 17, 3/4.

Pokrovskii, V.V. and Mozharova, G.I. (1991), 'Otsenka otnoshcheniia podraskov k probleme SPID', *Sovetskoe zdravookhranenie*, No. 6.

Polozhov, G. (1984), 'The problem teenager', cited in *Current Digest of the Soviet Press*, 36 (31).

Pritchard, C. et al. (1986), 'Incidence of drug and solvent use in "normal" fourth and fifth year comprehensive school children - some socio-behavioural characteristics', *British Journal of Social Work* 16.

Raska, E. (1978), 'Profil' zhiznennykh orientatsii kak sub"ektivnyi faktor prestupnosti molodezhi', *Sovetskoe Pravo*, No. 3.

Redhead, S. (ed) (1993), *Rave Off: Politics and Deviance in Contemporary Youth Culture*, Avebury, Aldershot.

Riordan, J. (1986), 'Growing pains of Soviet youth', *Journal of Communist Studies* Vol. 2, No. 2.

Riordan, J. (1987), 'Soviet youth culture', Paper presented to BASEES Annual Conference, Fitzwilliam College, Cambridge.

Riordan, J. (1989), *Soviet Youth Culture*, Macmillan, London.

Riordan, J. (1992), 'Soviet youth' in Lane, D. (ed), *Russia in Flux: The Political and Social Consequences of Reform*, Edward Elgar, Aldershot.

Riordan, J. (1993), 'Introduction' to Kon, I. and Riordan, J. (eds), *Sex and Russian Society*, Pluto Press, London.

Riordan, J. and Bridger, S. (eds) (1992), *Dear Comrade Editor: Readers' Letters to the Soviet Press Under Perestroika*, Indiana University Press, Bloomington.

Robertson, B.J. and McQueen, D.V. (1993), 'Conceptions and mis-conceptions about transmission of HIV/AIDS among the Scottish general public, 1988-1992', *Health Bulletin* Vol. 51, 5 September.

Roitman, L. (1978), 'SSSR, alkogoli i deti', *Nov. Russk. Slovo* 22 September.

Ryan, M. (1990), *Contemporary Soviet Society: A Statistical Handbook*, Edward Elgar, Aldershot.

Sakwa, R. (1993), *Russian Politics and Society*, Routledge, London.

Schaeffer Conroy, M. (1990), 'Abuse of drugs other than alcohol and tobacco in the Soviet Union', *Soviet Studies* Vol. 42, No. 3, July.

Segal, B. (1990), *The Drunken Society: Alcohol Abuse and Alcoholism in the Soviet Union - A Comparative Study*, Hippocrene Books, New York.

Shalatonova, I. et al. (1975), 'Shto pokazal opros potrebitelei tabachnykh izdelii', *Tabak*, No. 3.

Shaw, C.R. and Mackay, H. (1942), *Juvenile Delinquency and Urban Areas*, Chicago University Press, Chicago.

Shelley, L.I. (1980), 'Crime and Delinquency in the Soviet Union', in: Pankhurst, J.G. and Sacks, M. (eds), *Contemporary Soviet Society: Sociological Perspectives*, Praeger, New York.

Shelley, L.I. (1988), 'Crime and Criminals in the USSR', in Sacks, M.P. and Pankhurst, J.G. (eds), *Understanding Soviet Society*, Unwin Hyman, Boston.

Shelley, L.I. (1991), 'Crime in the Soviet Union', in Jones, A. et al. (eds), *Soviet Social Problems*, Westview Press, Boulder.

Skolnick, J. (1966), *Justice without Trial*, Wiley, New York.

Smirnov, V. (1985), 'Juvenile crime - Some statistics and Explanations', cited in *Current Digest of the Soviet Press,* 37 (6).

Social and Managerial Aspects of Economic Restructuring Survey (1993), Minsk.

Sokolov, V. (1986), *The Sociology of Moral Development of the Individual*, Minsk.

Strunin, L. and Hingson, R. (1987), 'AIDS and adolescents: Knowledge, belief, attitudes and behaviours', *Pediatrics,* 79.

Sutherland, E. (1947), *White Collar Crime*, Dryden Press, New York.

Swadi, H. (1988), 'Drug and substance use among 3,333 London adolescents', *British Journal of Addiction,* 83.

Sykes, G. and Mazda, D. (1961), *The Sociology of Crime and Delinquency*, Wiley, London.

Taylor, P. (1985), *The Smoke Ring: Tobacco, Money and International Politics*, Sphere Books, London.

Tedder, Iu. and Sidorova, P.I. (1976), 'Vliyanie sem'i na otnoshchenie detei k potrebleniiu spiritnykh napitkov', *Zdravookhranenie Rossiskoi Federatsii,* No. 7.

Timms, N.A. (1967), *Sociological Approach to Social Problems*, Routledge & Kegan Paul, London.

Titarenko, L. (1989), *The Political Culture of Young People*, Minsk.

Treml, V.G. (1975), 'Alcohol in the USSR: a fiscal dilemma', *Soviet Studies* Vol. 27, April.

Treml, V.G. (1982a), 'Deaths from alcoholic poisoning in the USSR', *Soviet Studies* Vol. 34, No. 4, October.

Treml, V.G. (1982b), *Alcohol in the USSR: A Statistical Study*, Duke University Press, Policy Studies, Durham NC.

Tretiy vserossisky syezd rossisskovo kommunisticheskovo soyuza molodozhi (1926), Moscow-Leningrad.

Urgent Problems of the Moral Upbringing of Students (1985), Minsk.

VII syezd Vsesoiuznovo Leninskovo soyuza molodozhi (1926), Moscow-Leningrad.

VKP (b) o Komsomole i molodyozhi: Sbornik reshiy i postanoveleniy partii o molodyozhi (1938), Moscow.

Volkov, B.S. and Lysov, M.D. (1983), *Pravpnarusheniia nesovershennoletnykh i ikh preduprezhdenie*, Kazan.

Vozhaki Komsomola: Sbornik (1978), Moscow.

Vsesoiuzny Leninsky kommunistichesky soyuz molodoyzni. Nadlyadnoye posobie (1985), Moscow.

Williams, C. (1986), 'The political economy of Health care in the USSR', unpublished MSc (Econ) thesis, CREES, University College Swansea, Wales, February.

Williams, C. (1991), 'Old habits die hard: Alcoholism in Leningrad under NEP and some lessons for the Gorbachov Administration', *Irish Slavonic Studies,* No. 12.

Williams, C. (1994), 'Sex education and the AIDS epidemic in the former Soviet Union', *Sociology of Health and Illness,* Vol. 16, No. 1, January.

Williams, C. (1995), *AIDS in Post-Communist Russia and its Successor States*, Avebury, Aldershot.

Yankelovich, D. (1974), *The New Morality: A Profile of American Youth in the 1970s*, McGraw-Hill, New York.

Young, J. (1971), *The Drugtakers*, Paladin, London.

Index